MAGICAL TALES

EMPIREVM
Decimum Coelum
Nonū Coelū
Octauum
COELV
SA

MAGICAL TALES

Myth, legend and enchantment in children's books

EDITED BY
CAROLYNE LARRINGTON & DIANE PURKISS

Bodleian Library
UNIVERSITY OF OXFORD

First published in 2013 by the Bodleian Library
Broad Street
Oxford OX1 3BG

www.bodleianbookshop.co.uk

ISBN 978 1 85124 264 1

Cover design by Lucy Morton at illuminati
Designed and typeset in 11 on 16 Jensen by illuminati, Grosmont
Printed and bound by Great Wall Printing Co. Ltd, Hong Kong
on Gold East 157 gsm matt art paper

British Library Catalogue in Publishing Data
A CIP record of this publication is available from the British Library

Contents

Foreword

Books open up the world of the imagination to children. Even before they can read, pop-up picture books surprise and delight them with their magical effects. And once children can read for themselves, books invite them into a space in which anything is possible. Not only fairies, gnomes and wizards, but talking mice, helpful squirrels and other more sinister creatures stalk the pages of children's literature, catching the child's imagination and pressing against the boundary between the possible and impossible, the mundane and the fantastic. Books offer children a kind of magical experience, and none more so than books for children which bring the ancient myths of the British Isles and the stories of the medieval past to life between their covers, or which redeploy medievalist themes in newly imagined worlds: Narnia, Middle Earth, Philip Pullman's alternative Oxford, even Hogwarts.

The magic *of* children's books and the magic *in* books often originates in a library. Within children's fictions these are the

THE
HOBBIT

by

J. R. R. Tolkien

mysterious dusty libraries which conceal on their shelves danger-ous books of knowledge and power. So too in the Bodleian Library itself, many of the nineteenth and twentieth century's most creative children's authors encountered the ancient stories of myth and magic which they retold, or which fired their imaginations to create the new fantasy worlds whose roots nevertheless run deep into the mythic and medieval past.

C.S. Lewis, J.R.R. Tolkien, Alan Garner, Philip Pullman, Diana Wynne Jones, Susan Cooper, Kevin Crossley-Holland: all these authors studied at Oxford and their hours spent in the Bodleian inspired their writings in countless ways. The exhibition which this book accompanies draws on the Library's extensive holdings of nineteenth- and twentieth-century children's books which allow us to trace the ways in which Anglo-Saxon, medieval, Norse, Celtic and Arthurian stories have been told and retold for children, and show us how such legends were reshaped in Narnia and Middle Earth, and formed the essential building-blocks for other imagina-tive universes. The Library's splendid collections of the medieval manuscripts with which Tolkien and Lewis worked in their careers as Oxford dons are also represented here, as are the treasures from the literary estates of Tolkien and Lewis, and the rich collection of papers and other materials from Alan Garner's archive.

Books inspire magical tales, but they can also teach the initiate how to perform magic. The Library has an outstanding collec-tion of manuscripts, rolls and early printed books which tell of alchemical secrets, mysterious charms and spells, or which list magical creatures and their habitats. The extraordinary Ripley rolls with their detailed plans of alchemical processes, the demonic manual of MS. Ashmole 1406 and the tiny secret manuscript of charms, MS. e Mus. 243, are all to be seen here, with other grimoires and bestiaries from the Library's collections. Children's books, especially early ones, could also be constructed with secret flaps, sudden pop-ups and hidden folds, performing magic for the surprised and delighted child and suggesting that magic was not lost in the ancient past, nor buried deep in arcane books; rather it is alive and weaving its spells in the present. The Bodleian is fortunate to house the Iona and Peter Opie Collection of Children's Literature, which has an unparalleled number of early children's movable books, and many of these are on display, along with some items from the John Johnson Collection of Printed Ephemera.

The Library is grateful to the English Faculty Library, Lady Margaret Hall, Manchester City Art Galleries, the Ashmolean Museum, the Museum of the History of Science, the British Museum, the British Library, the National Portrait Gallery, the Tolkien and Lewis estates, Alan Garner, Marvel Comics, and Haukur Halldórsson for illustrations, permissions and loans. These are acknowledged individually in the book's chapters.

We are also grateful for the excellent work of the Exhibitions Team at the Bodleian, led by Madeline Slaven, and to Dr Samuel Fanous and the staff of Bodleian Publications. The Bodleian's exhibitions and associated publications develop in conjunction with academics working in the University, and with scholars elsewhere. Dr Judith Priestman and Sarah Wheale from the Bodleian Libraries Department of Special Collections have curated the exhibition drawing freely on ideas presented by the authors of the individual chapters, Diane Purkiss, Carolyne Larrington, David Clark, Anna Caughey and Hannah Field, thus uniting Oxford's renowned collections and its research activities in a fruitful synergy.

Sarah E. Thomas
Bodley's Librarian

Introduction

CAROLYNE LARRINGTON WITH DIANE PURKISS

Books are magical. Even the infant who gazes in wonder at the pop-up picture book with its hidden secrets and surprises registers that something special is happening before its eyes and crows in delight. The very first reading books that children encounter are crammed with magic: princesses, fairies, knights and wizards, dwarves and dragons throng their pages. Alongside the mundane world of trains and tractors, of mummies and daddies, there exists an imaginative space in which animals can talk, children can fly, and, crucially, in which the monsters sometimes *do* come out from under the bed. Children's imaginations are kindled by magical thinking, by their willingness to believe in other kinds of worlds, in past or future places, where the parameters of this world are explored and tested.

The older child too finds magic between the covers of books. Not just the magic of fairies and wizards, of vampires and werewolves – though these remain central themes in young adult and crossover fiction – but, more importantly, the magic of the act of reading itself. Books transport children out of the everyday surroundings in which they read, away from the bedroom, or the bus, or the living-room floor, into an intensely realised other place where what is read becomes somehow more real than reality itself. Books open that magical door to Narnia, or Middle Earth, to Alan Garner's Alderley Edge or J.K. Rowling's Hogwarts. In a recessive move familiar to every reader, old or young, the child protagonists of children's literature themselves venture into dusty libraries or gloomy book-lined studies. Here they open mysterious, yet enticing, books, encased in strange bindings and written in curious characters. These books work magic on the reading hero, for good or ill, endowing the inquisitive with undreamt-of powers, tempting them with forbidden

2 Fragment of *The Lion, the Witch and the Wardrobe*.

Oxford, Bodleian Library, MS. Eng. misc. c. 1109, fol. iv. Extracts/images © copyright C.S. Lewis Pte Ltd.

This book is about four children whose names were Ann, Martin, Rose and Peter. But it is most about Peter who was the youngest. They all had to go away from London suddenly because of Air Raids, and because Father, who was in the Army, had gone off to the war and Mother was doing some kind of war work. They were sent to stay with a kind of relation of Mother's who was a very old Professor who lived all by himself in the country delights and offering chances to meddle with the narrative's realities. Books within books must be respected, for they are both enabling and dangerous.

And when the last page is turned and the book is put aside with a wistful sigh – or is begun all over again – the growing reader looks for new stories, other kinds of magic. Every children's author recalls in his or her work that absorbed, hungrily reading child that they once were, and the stories that delighted them. Children's writers continue to interact with the imaginative world of childhood which they have long left behind, and yet which stays with them always. Magic in books comes pre-eminently out of other books. When C.S. Lewis set out to write his prequel to *The Lion, the Witch and the Wardrobe*, we see him drawing on his and his brother's childhood fantasy world of Boxen, a world where children and animals could converse. That early world grew out of Lewis's love of Beatrix Potter's *Tale of Squirrel Nutkin*, a book which for Lewis always conjured the complex feelings of autumn. Here is an early version of Digory Kirke, standing in a garden in London, but a garden contemporary with the wartime setting of *The Lion*, and talking to a red squirrel called Pattertwig, who can understand him and respond (*figure 3*). A false start? Perhaps; Lewis did not take this version of the story forward, but it was simmering in his mind and clearly informed what he eventually wrote. That lonely boy with mean relatives and only the animals for company eventually became Prince Caspian, and Lewis kept the red squirrel Pattertwig in that novel.

for ever so long?"

"I've been ill," said Digory.

"You humans are always being ill," said the squirrel, "you're as bad as the cattle. Would you like a nut?"

"Are you sure you can spare it, Pattertwig?" said Digory, "Now that the winter's coming on and all?"

"P-r-r-r," chattered the squirrel contemptuously, "What do you take me for? A nice sort of squirrel I should be if I hadn't got a pile big enough to spare a nut to a friend without missing it."

"But you were saying last time we met how hard times were getting," protested Digory. Pattertwig, however, made no answer for he had already jumped from the Oak to the Birch and from the Birch to the Fir and was off to fetch the nut. Digory at once looked the other way; it is considered very manners among squirrels to watch anyone going to his hoard. To ask where it is would be simply outrageous.

"Aren't you going to talk to me?" said the Birch in its silvery, showery, rustling voice.

"Of course I am," replied Digory. "In fact I was coming down to have a dance with you in a moment."

"No good to-day," said the Birch. "I can't dance when

3 **The Lefay fragment,** an abandoned 'prequel' to *The Lion, the Witch and the Wardrobe*. It is named after Mrs Lefay, Digory's godmother. Here Digory meets Pattertwig the squirrel.

Digory's unusual name may have been an updating of Degaré;
the romance of Sir Degaré, featuring a princess, an elf-prince and
a sundered family, was a tale Lewis encountered in his studies at
Oxford (*figure* 4). He and his friend J.R.R. Tolkien found their
inspiration for new stories in the real-life versions of the libraries
and studies which contain and conceal magical books in children's
tales. As professors of medieval literature at Oxford, Lewis and
Tolkien immersed themselves in Anglo-Saxon and Old Norse

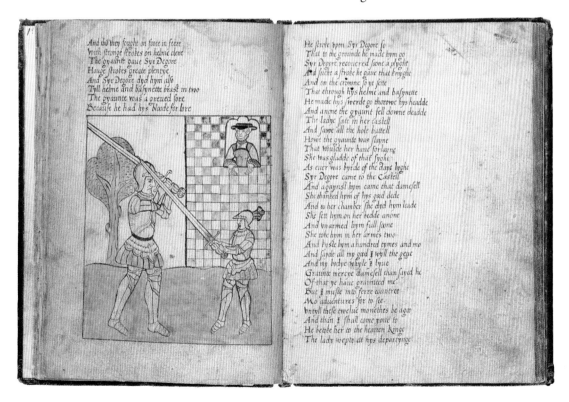

5 The scorched and damaged Book of Mazarbul from *The Lord of the Rings*, as imagined by Tolkien.

6 A fragment of an Anglo-Saxon manuscript burnt in the famous Ashburnham House fire of 1731. This destroyed a large number of Anglo-Saxon manuscripts from the Cotton Library collection.

Oxford, Bodleian Library, MS. Rawl. Q. e. 20.

literature, in romance and religious poetry, and their teaching and research renewed and stimulated their childhood memories of magical worlds and mythical places. So we find J.R.R. Tolkien creating his images of the Book of Mazarbul, the fragments of which were found by Gandalf and the Company of the Ring in the depths of Moria. Tolkien gives the book burned leaves and a text which is only partly preserved (*figure 5*). The damaged and fragmented reality of the book of Mazarbul lends a truth to the whole passage's evocation of last stands and lost kingdoms. More, it shows us Tolkien's preoccupation with the terrible vulnerability of culture and civilisation to war, to accident, to mortality. Placing the book Tolkien made alongside one of the Anglo-Saxon manuscript fragments scorched in the Cotton Library fire (*figure 6*), we see why he was inspired to make his own torn and smoky copy of written treasure.

Stories of King Arthur or of the gods and heroes of the North were not only mediated through the romances and sagas which Lewis, Tolkien and their pupils studied, but also by high and popular culture. Music, such as the operas of Richard Wagner, Pre-Raphaelite paintings of Arthurian subjects, and engravings made to illustrate popular or translated versions of the great legends profoundly influenced writers' emotional understanding. The teenage C.S. Lewis suddenly encountered what he would later call 'Pure Northernness' when he accidentally caught sight of one of Arthur Rackham's illustrations for Wagner's *Ring* in the Christmas issue of the magazine *The Bookman* (*figure 7*).

7 Arthur Rackham's illustration of Siegfried and the Rhinemaidens from *Götterdämmerung*. This was the image which fired the young C.S. Lewis's imagination with the idea of 'pure Northernness'. The Rhinemaidens beg Siegfried to return the Ring to them and warn of his impending doom.

Oxford, Bodleian Library, Per. 25805 c.2 (October 1911–March 1912) vol. XLI, illustration between pages 144 & 145.

Pure 'Northernness' engulfed me: a vision of huge, clear spaces hanging above the Atlantic in the endless twilight of Northern summer, remoteness, severity … and almost at the same moment I knew that I had met this before, long, long ago. … And with that plunge back into my own past, there arose at once, almost like heartbreak, the memory of Joy itself, the knowledge that I had once had what I had now lacked for years, that I was returning at last from exile and desert lands to my own country, and the distance of the Twilight of the Gods and the distance of my own past Joy, both unattainable, flowed together in a single, unendurable sense of desire and loss.[1]

The picture and the words, the enticingly lovely Rhinemaidens beckoning to the hero Siegfried, and the evocative name of the opera, *Götterdämmerung* ('Twilight of the Gods') nourished a longing for something whose name Lewis did not then know or understand, but which would later take shape as Narnia. Tolkien too writes of 'Joy, Joy beyond the walls of the world, poignant as grief' in his essay *On Fairy Stories*.[2] Later authors who studied English literature at Oxford University, the 'Oxford School' of children's writers, following the syllabus which Tolkien and Lewis devised, studied Old and Middle English and Old Norse literature as part of their course. Diana Wynne Jones, Susan Cooper, Alan Garner, Philip Pullman and Kevin Crossley-Holland are among the writers who found inspiration in stories which were already ancient when they were related in the medieval past. Their imaginative worlds have been inflected by the myths and legends they encountered there.

Magical books do not exist only *within* books however. Words of power, abracadabras and charms, intended to bend reality and change the visible world, complex alchemical apparatuses designed to harness cosmic powers to bring new substances into being and manuals of demonic secrets were written down and preserved within the great scholarly libraries of Europe over many centuries. The Bodleian Library houses many such vellums and rolls, bearing witness to the eternal human desire to penetrate the arcane and master the unseen. Such strange and dark texts seem far removed from the harmless magic-performing books of early childhood with their panoramas and pop-ups, and yet they too inspire chidren's authors and child-readers with their glimpses of the kinds of secrets that the world tries to hide from innocence.

This book explores myth and magic in children's literature from around 1800 to the present day. Diane Purkiss's chapter charts the magic of the magical book in children's stories, the dangers and the delights which lurk between the covers of the texts that lead the child protagonist into astonishing adventures, endowing them with powers beyond their years and anticipating some of the difficulties and dilemmas which maturity will bring. Purkiss also discusses some of the 'real' magical books which inspired such authors as Alan Garner: charm collections, alchemical rolls and manuals of demonic magic. Carolyne Larrington traces the growing interest in Norse mythology in the nineteenth and twentieth centuries, showing how the myths of Odin, Thor and Freyja, and the legend of the hero Sigurd have been reshaped for generations of children. David Clark discusses the ways in which the Anglo-Saxon and high medieval past and its traditions inspired writers from George

Macdonald through to today's authors. He looks closely at the 'Oxford School', whose style of medievalism was shaped by the strongly medieval-inflected literature course which the Oxford English Faculty provided until the mid-1970s, and whose influence on the imaginations of later writers such as J.K. Rowling can be clearly seen. Anna Caughey's chapter explores the revival of Arthurian medievalism in the nineteenth century. Arthur and his knights embodied ideals of chivalry which trained generations of boys to become both gentlemen and servants of empire, yet the potency of the Arthurian tradition has survived both the loss of empire and the social revolutions of the last century, constantly revisited and renewed in children's stories. Finally, Hannah Field explores the ways in which children's books could literally perform magic for the young reader; clever technological innovations in paper, card and printing made magical effects possible. Nursery rhymes and fairy stories, wizards and stage-magician conjuring, provided ideal frameworks and storylines for the publishers to show off their new techniques. Such literal magic books initiate the very youngest readers, those who would grow into older child readers, and ultimately, perhaps, the adult writers of new stories, into the magical world of children's books.

I

Books of magic

'The best kind of book,' said Barnaby, 'is a magic book.'

'Naturally,' said John.

… Barnaby opened his top book and began chapter one. But after only a paragraph or two he leafed over to the back, glanced at the last pages, and shut the cover with a disgusted bang.

'I thought so,' he said. 'Of all the gyps! It calls itself *The Magic Door*, but there's not a speck of real magic in it anywhere! It's just about this boy that learns to get along with these other people by being friendly and stuff. And the magic door's just the door of good fellowship or something. Man, do I despise a book like that!'[1]

IN this passage from *Seven-Day Magic* (1962), Edward Eager reminds us of the see-sawing hopes of children; the hope of finding a book that will act as a portal from the boring everyday into a new and shining world of magic. He also reminds us that unscrupulous adults are willing to exploit the child's longings in order to smuggle in a moral message. The tension between the wish-fulfilment of books that sweep a child away from the relative powerlessness and constraint of reality and the warning that constraint and disapproval accompany power is central to the portrayal of magic books in children's fantasy fiction.

In one sense, all books are magic books; even a dystopian novel set in the slums of New York has the power to whisk us away from our own lives, endowing us with abilities we have never possessed. As long as the child remains inside the book, he or she remains powerful. To be inside the book, though, you have to believe in the book. You have to be immersed in it, to feel as if it's happening all round you. Ironically, this means the book itself has to vanish. Lines of print can act like cages, keeping magic away, getting between the reader and the scene. For the magic to work, the book must absent itself. However, while all books are magic, some are more magical than others, in that some are actually books of spells, theurgy and learned invocation. Appearing often in children's fantasy, such books represent a fascination with books themselves. In this chapter, I will examine the power of the magical book in two ways. First, and primarily, I will look at ways in which books which actually contain magical spells or books are portrayed in children's literature, focusing in the main on authors who have a connection with Oxford and Oxford University. Second, I will look at the one author who actually does use medieval and early modern spellbooks as a source for his fiction of magic.

Magic that uses words and writing has a history which goes back to the era before the codex. Magical papyri containing curses or charms survive from every civilisation of any size of the pre-Christian world, and while the Church was uneasy with such works, they survived into the Christian era, often circulating through oral learning or in manuscript, and only entering print after the Restoration. Grimoires – a useful term for books containing magic spells – and such books are not, however, the main or only sources for the magical book motif in children's literature. Such books more often represent imaginative extensions of ideas of power and capability rather than the kinds of spells magical books actually contain. Other books draw on myth and legend to allocate powers beyond the human. The focus here, however, is on texts which understand the written or the printed word as a key to magical power, and which incorporate that magic into stories, thus in the majority of cases using the motif of the grimoire from history without using its content. Magic which is not derived from or embodied in books I leave for others; I also leave aside magic derived from folklore, which finds little place in the portrayal of books of magic since those represent a more literate and literary tradition. Other chapters in this book deal with the use of mythic sources, while here I focus not on sources, but on differing thematic images of books of magic.

Lucy Pevensie and her brother Edmund are on a voyage on the Narnian ship *Dawn Treader* (1952) when they make landfall on an island inhabited by invisible beings, beings who insist that Lucy rescue them from their invisibility. This involves reading a spell from a magic book housed in the study of the enigmatic magician. Fearfully, Lucy makes her way down a long corridor to the magician's library. She is further unnerved by mysterious signs

on the walls, and by the appearance of a strange mirror, which frames her face in a beard; the bearded glass seems to transform Lucy into an adult male magician. The library is full of books – 'more books than Lucy had ever seen before, tiny little books, fat and dumpy books, and books bigger than any church Bible you have ever seen, all bound in leather and smelling old and learned and magical'.[2] But Lucy knows the Magic Book is the one lying on a desk. She has to find a particular spell in it, which means she has to read it from the beginning; there is no index and no table of contents.

The book is clearly medieval in style with its clasp binding, lack of a title page, and handwriting, 'written, not printed; written in a clear, even hand, with thick downstrokes and thin upstrokes'.[3]

8 Alchemical lion image from a fifteenth-century magic scroll.

Oxford, Bodleian Library, MS. Bodl. Rolls 1.

The spells in the book are lavishly illustrated by pictures which not only come to life, but become personal and particular. The whole book is a mirror held up to Lucy. When Lucy begins noticing spells that might have some personal use for her, the one which attracts her most is 'An infallible spell to make beautiful her that uttereth it beyond the lot of mortals.' Here, the book comes to be Lucy's fantasy-daydream of what life would be like if she said the spell. 'Beyond the lot of mortals' is a moral red flag. Mortals are not supposed to try to achieve the status of gods by using magic. Critics tend to want to discuss the moment in relation to Lucy's jealousy of her prettier sister Susan, and this is an element, but moreover Susan is Lucy's image of what it will be like to be beautiful and successful and the object of the jealousy of others. Lewis also alludes to the Trojan War, in which half-divine Helen, beautiful beyond the lot of mortals, is the cause of ten years of fighting and slaughter. So too it can be for Lucy: 'it turned from tournaments to real wars, and all Narnia and Archenland, Telmar and Calormen, Galma and Terebinthia, were laid waste with the fury of the kings and dukes and great lords who fought for her favour.'[4] In his manuscript draft 'After Ten Years', Lewis refers to the problem of Helen, but points out that she will have aged; all female claims to beauty are subject to time (*figure* 9). 'In reading great literature I become a thousand men and yet remain myself', wrote Lewis in *An Experiment in Criticism*.[5] This is exactly Lucy's experience reading the magician's book. She is Lucy Pevensie, with an older sister prettier than she, and she is Helen of Troy, who

Yellowhead

"Steady, men," said Menelaus. "Don't go inside yet; get your breath." Then in a lower voice "Get in the doorway, Eteoneus, and don't let them in. We don't want them to start looting yet."

It was less than two hours since they had left the horse, and all had gone extremely well. They had had no difficulty in finding the Scaean gate. Once you are inside a city's wall every unarmed enemy is ~~dead or alive~~ either a guide or a dead man and must choose to be the first. There was a guard at the gate, of course, but they had disposed of it quickly and, what was best of all, with very little ~~noise~~. In twenty minutes they had got the gate open and the main army was pouring in. There had been no serious fighting till they reached the citadel. It had been lively enough there for a bit, but Yellowhead and his Spartans had suffered little, because Agamemnon had insisted on leading the van. Yellowhead had thought, all things considered, that this place should have been his own, for the whole war was in a sense his war, even if Agamemnon were the king of kings and his elder brother. Once they were inside the ~~main~~ outer circling wall of the citadel, the main body had set about the inner gate which was very strong, while Yellowhead and his party had been sent round to find a back way in. They had overpowered what defence they found there and now they stopped to pant and wipe their faces and clean their swords and spears. Blades.

This little porch opened on a stone platform circled by a wall that was only breast-high. Yellowhead leaned his elbow on it and looked down. He could not see the citadel now. Troy was burning. The glorious fires, the loud manes and beards of flame and the billows of smoke, blotted out the sky. Beyond the city the whole countryside was lit up with the glare; you would see even the familiar and hateful beach itself and the endless ~~line~~ line of ships. Thank the gods, they would soon bid good-bye to that!

While they had been fighting he had never given Helen a thought and had been happy; he had felt himself once more a king and a soldier, and every decision he made had proved right. As the sweat dried, though, he was thirsty; an oven and ~~had~~ a smarting little gash ~~above~~ above his knee, some of the sweetness of victory began to ooze ~~into~~ out of his mind. Agamemnon no doubt would be called the city-sacker. But Yellowhead had a notion that when the story reached the minstrels he himself would be the centre of it. The ~~chance~~ pith of the song would be how Menelaus king of Sparta had won back from

9 Draft manuscript of 'After Ten Years', Lewis's unfinished novel about Troy and Helen.

Oxford, Bodleian Library, Dep. d. 247, fol. 69r. Extracts/images © copyright C.S. Lewis Pte Ltd.

launched a thousand ships. This is not just about temptation, then, but about the particular seduction of reading. If I become an evildoer while reading, do I then become evil myself? Yet all that prevents Lucy from saying the spell is the growling face of Aslan, which materialises among the opening words of the spell, a visible conscience.

We have flicked hastily past the spell for toothache (which appears near the beginning of the Magic Book), and yet Lewis was suffering from toothache while his mother was dying. He was ten years old, and he was calling for her, and she didn't come because she herself was dying. Are spells what we promise ourselves in such moments of defeated grief as Lewis experienced then? Magic gives us what we cannot get (endless gold, endless food, endless beauty, endless life) and it does what we cannot even imagine. It doesn't fill a hole in us; it makes us new. So, for Lewis, the idea of the magic book's existence and the child's discovery of it are both invested with the power to overcome the griefs of human life, because it contains what his dying mother could not give him: a spell to make it *all be*tter. The magician's book probably seems male, owned by a male magician and inhabited by protective but authoritarian Aslan, but in this revelation we see that it can be maternal too.

In a way the point of magic for children is that it offers them power normally assumed by them to be confined to adults. In magic books, power becomes accessible, and can be redistributed, overcoming hierarchies that may exclude them. Through magic books, child characters gain power via magic in relation to adults, and in relation to one another. Magic in fantasy for children is not the redistribution of wealth, but the redistribution of hope. All hierarchical societies need to be careful to ensure hope is evenly distributed. Magic is the narrative equivalent of the lottery; if you are singled out, if you are special, then you can *suddenly* be transformed from humble girl in rags into ball-gowned princess, from lonely orphan into famous hero, from plain sister into raving beauty as Lucy hopes and wishes. Just as a child might choose a book from a long shelf of possibilities, so that child can choose a spell that will change everything. You could become anything – an animal, a monster, a princess, a superhero – by using the right spell.

Magic books require something from their users. They are not simply devices; they need to be read, searched, analysed, decoded, learned like languages and lovingly perused like comics. There is always the hope of finding a book with spells in it that really work. These longings are not necessarily childish; they were shared by medieval and Renaissance magicians and their clients, men who fastened on the spurious works of the god-magician 'Hermes Trismegistus', or on the lost magic books of Dr Dee. The monastic libraries, literally ripped apart at the Dissolution, became the focus of legends of lost magic books coming to light in the ruins of old abbeys, and ancient libraries such as the Bodleian Library became spaces where scholars hoped to find something left undeciphered by previous generations' searches, perhaps among the books of Elias Ashmole or John Aubrey. Ashmole and Aubrey themselves

10 C.S. Lewis by
Walter Stoneman, 1955.

© National Portrait Gallery,
London.

shared those fantasies of finding a lost manuscript that would provide the key to everything. In the past, when literacy was unusual, the very possession of books could make their owner seem powerful, even frightening. Written words allow knowledge to be passed on to new generations. Magic is often about discovering something long lost or forgotten. The codex – the book with covers which can be shut tight – can be a place for secrets. Magic can lie concealed in an ordinary-looking book – in endpapers, in a folded paper inside something dull.

In children's fiction, magic books are often secret, as in Susan Cooper's *The Dark Is Rising* (1973). Such ancient secrets can be preserved for a particular recipient, inherited or saved from the wreck of the past. The reading of such books is pivotal, transforming ordinary childhood into fantasy adventure. In *The Dark Is Rising*, Will Stanton needs the book of *gramarye* to seize his destiny and become an Old One. In a section of the novel entitled 'The Learning', Will reads the book:

> 'This is the oldest book in the world,' [Merriman] said simply. 'And when you have read it, it will be destroyed. This is the Book of Gramarye, written in the Old Speech. It cannot be understood by any except the Old Ones, and even if a man or creature might understand any spell of power that it contains, he could not use their words of power unless he were an Old One himself.[6]

The book is overpoweringly old. It has been kept especially for Will. It is in a language only a special cadre of people can understand. It is extraordinarily secret, and that makes it believable.

Will's reading gives him the power to fly, to master all the elements; the book unreels in his hands like a film, tiny fragments of poetry – including a line from Tennyson's 'The Eagle' – expand into vast historical landscapes. Its very abstruseness implies that knowledge of such power may lie concealed in other books, dispersed and unrecognised. Its age is attested by the way it concludes with a line from the final Branch of the Welsh *Mabinogi*, containing a reference to Math ap Mathonwy, the magician who makes a wife out of flowers for the cursed king Lleu Llaw Gyffes. Cooper does not mention this terrible story, though it will be familiar to readers of Alan Garner's *The Owl Service* (1967), but it represents an overmastering magic, one which goes beyond the bounds with disastrous results. This correlates with Cooper's general unease with magical powers. 'It is a responsibility, a heaviness.'[7] In using the book Will becomes unwittingly complicit in a cruel, unjust exploitation of a relation between a master and his servant. The servant, Hawkin, has been forced to risk his life to keep the book safe, and when he realises that his master is willing to let him die if necessary, he betrays the master's cause. Is even the most esoteric knowledge worth a life? Cooper does not linger over the question, but she does pose it.

One way of burying knowledge is encoding it in lost languages, or in untranslatable and unmanageable fragments of the past. The name is power. Some children's authors have drawn on this idea extensively, such as Ursula Le Guin in her Earthsea series (1968–2003), in which the name in dragon speech is the truth of the person's identity. Saying a true name gives a wizard power over identity, over ostensibly bigger or stronger foes. Names and words are magic to children in any case. As Le Guin herself writes in her creative writing manual *Steering the Craft*:

> Most children enjoy the sound of language for its own sake. They wallow in repetitions and luscious word-sounds and the crunch and slither of onomatopoeia; they fall in love with musical or impressive words and use them in all the wrong places.[8]

The idea that language's pulsions are a childhood pleasure that can be remembered in maturity recurs in the magic of the Earthsea books. The point of magical language is that it is not entirely cognitive; it is about the aspects of language which cannot be reduced to clear meanings and denotations. Here is Prince Arren, hearing the dragon language:

> he was on the point of understanding, almost understanding; as if it were a language he had forgotten, not one he had never known. In speaking it the mage's voice was much clearer than when he spoke Hardic, and seemed to make a kind of silence around it, as does the softest touch on a great bell. But the dragon's voice was like a gong, both deep and shrill, or the hissing thrum of cymbals.[9]

This is of course how very small children experience language before they can speak it. For J.R.R. Tolkien, too, fairy stories were a way to recover a place of lost play, through a forgotten language: 'It was in fairy-stories that I first divined the potency of the words … [in] that sense only a taste for [fairy stories] may make us, or keep us, childish.'[10]

11 J.R.R. Tolkien, 1911.
Oxford, Bodleian Library, MS. Tolkien photogr. 4, fol. 16.

Conversely, there might also be fear. The 'magic' of language is its power of ordering experience and providing the possibility of meaning. The true death, the end of the world which threatens in *The Farthest Shore* (1972), is the loss of language, the death of art. The really terrifying aspect of this last novel is not the journey of Arren and Ged through the kingdom of death, but the 'vision of a languageless world'.[11] In Earthsea, the impression the dragon speech makes is at least in part dependent on the fact that Arren does not know what it means. Magic often involves unknown tongues, or tongues that were known once but are now forgotten. Latin, Ancient Greek, names in Hebrew … even nonsense words like Abracadabra. The origin of this word is disputed, but it is found in post-classical Latin as early as the second century and in English from 1565. Although its etymology is obscure, it may be related to *abecedarium* (abecedary – meaning *alphabetical*).[12] Many medieval grimoires also feature Latin spells and non-existent words, perhaps representing the half-understood languages overheard in childhood.

The interplay of indulgence and rebuke is something that comes to children's literature from the Western magical tradition itself, though it is amplified by concerns about children's moral development. As a result, not all magic books are portrayed in positive terms. This may be especially true when the book is not a tool which allows the child to do magic, but instead acts on its own, usually to exert its magical power on the child. In Diana Wynne Jones's *The Magicians of Caprona* (1980), magic is commonplace, but children are still enticed and almost killed by a magic book. This is not a book of magic spells, but a book that is itself magical:

> It was the most gripping story Tonino had ever read. It started with the boy, Giorgio, going along a mysterious alleyway near the docks on his way home from school. There was a peeling blue house at the end of the alley, and, just as Giorgio passed it, a scrap of paper fluttered from one of its windows.[13]

Like a literary tourist, Tonino is compelled to follow in the footsteps of his fictional hero and counterpart, but the book as a whole turns out to be a powerful calling charm, and when he reaches the house from the story he is kidnapped by the book's villain. Tonino's reading is clearly dangerous because it is so obviously gratifying, such a clear ego massage.

The very freedom of access and democratisation of knowledge which magic books promise can become a threat if the child protagonist tries to exceed his or her hierarchical limits with the help of such books. This motif is potent in 'The Sorcerer's Apprentice', originally a poem by Goethe (1797).[14] In Earthsea, magic books can cause magic users to run amok. The young Ged first encounters a spell in his old master Ogion's book:

> As he read it, puzzling out the runes and symbols one by one, a horror came over him. His eyes were fixed, and he could not lift them till he had finished reading all the spell.
>
> Then raising his head he saw it was dark in the house. He had been reading without any light, in the darkness. He could not now make out the runes when he looked down at the book. Yet the

horror grew in him, seeming to hold him bound in his chair. He was cold. Looking over his shoulder he saw that something was crouching beside the closed door, a shapeless clot of shadow darker than the darkness.[15]

The young boy is saved by his master, but this is a spell which Ged is doomed to reprise later, with near-fatal consequences. He is punished for his presumption. In Diane Duane's *So You Want to Be a Wizard* (1982), Nita's sister tries frantically to cure her mother's cancer, but she has burned herself out misusing magic, and can no longer muster the necessary powers. She has wasted her abilities on trivia. Structurally, this story is disturbingly like Maria Edgeworth's story 'The Purple Jar' (first printed 1796), in which a child wastes her money on a jar which turns out not to be magical but merely full of purple liquid, and is punished by being made to do without shoes. The structural parallelism makes it clear that magic in stories often represents the power of money to acquire and to command, a power often reserved for adults.

Sometimes, a book of magic is just precisely what is needed, tailored to the child characters who consult it. In Victoria Walker's *The Winter of Enchantment* (1969), the evil magician's book actively helps the children by answering all their questions. Melissa discovers the book in the enchanter's library: 'I was running my fingers along the back of those books over there, when I felt one which was warm. All the others on either side were quite cold. … It felt quite different from the others.'[16] The book belongs to an evil enchanter, but Melissa and Sebastian are allowed to use it with impunity. In *So You Want to Be a Wizard*, Nita's adventures also begin in a library, and Duane makes it clear that Nita's reading has primed her to seek a more exciting world:

> Strange creatures like phoenixes and psammeads, moving under smoky London daylight of a hundred years before, in company with groups of bemused children; starships and new worlds and the limitless vistas of interstellar night, outer space challenged but never conquered; princesses in silver and golden dresses; princes and heroes carrying swords like sharpened lines of light, monsters rising out of weedy tarns, wild creatures that talked and tricked one another.…
>
> *I used to think the world would be like that when I got older. Wonderful all the time, exciting, happy. Instead of the way it is…*[17]

After these reflections, Nita happens on a different book:

> Something stopped Nita's hand as it ran along the bookshelf. She looked and found that one of the books, a little library-bound volume in shiny red buckram, had a loose thread at the top of its spine, on which her finger had caught. She pulled the finger free, glanced at the title. It was one of those So You Want to Be a … books, a series on careers. *So You Want to Be a Pilot* there had been, and *So You Want to Be a Scientist … a Nurse … a Writer…*
>
> But this one said, *So You Want to Be a Wizard*.[18]

Nita is good at magic because she is interested in words and descriptions, and these readerly characteristics turn out to be prerequisites for magic too. In Diana Wynne Jones's *Witch Week* (1982), Nan's mesmeric storytelling is vital for the most important act of magic in the book. These stories subtly compliment the child reader, allowing him or her to think of him- or herself as a potential magician awaiting discovery.

Duane's is one of many instances of books that recognise and attach themselves to the child for whom they are destined. In Michelle Lovric's *The Undrowned Child* (2009), Teodora does not so much find a very old book as be found by one; the magic book throws itself at her head, knocking her unconscious. The shopkeeper gives her the book, which has no title, but has a picture of a mermaid on the front, a mermaid who comes to life and winks at Teodora. When she opens the book, she finds her own name inside, in a script already brown with age. The book says that it has been waiting for her. Teodora is an example of a child destined for a special life, framed as a child recognisable from an ancient prophecy; a similar story is told about Lyra Belacqua in Philip Pullman's *His Dark Materials* trilogy (1995–2000), though Lyra does not read a book but an aleitheiometer. Such special children often have their specialness confirmed by an encounter with a book they can master more easily than others can. In Garth Nix's *Lirael* (2001), Lirael is destined to be the next Abhorsen, but discovers this only by reading *The Book of the Dead* all night: 'she felt it [the book] recognised her lack of knowledge'.[19]

The child and the book can be or can become one in these stories. The idea that a book has a mind of its own and the idea that the child-imagination is potentially magical combine to conjure the idea of a magic book which *is* the child. In Terry Pratchett's *Hogfather* (1996), each individual may find themselves in the library of Death: 'Everyone, it is said, has a book inside them. In this library, everyone was inside a book ... a scribble

12 Duke Humfrey's Library, Oxford. This is the oldest reading room in the Bodleian Library. It was used as the fictional setting for one part of the library at Hogwarts in the film adaptations of *Harry Potter*.

of handwriting following the narrative of every life.'[20] Children's books often soft-pedal or demonise such identities, however. J.K. Rowling does the latter when the diary of Tom Riddle possesses the soul of Ginny Weasley, and has to be ritually slain.

Sometimes, the title of the published book deliberately mirrors the title of the magical book in the story. In Cornelia Funke's *Inkheart* (2003), Meggie's father has the power to bring characters from any book to life by reading the book aloud, and he accidentally 'reads' the child's mother into a book – called *Inkheart*. In Matthew Skelton's *Endymion Spring* (2006), Blake and Duck come across a strange book in a library in Oxford, which is entitled *Endymion Spring*. This implies that the purchased book somehow confers some of the powers of its magical cognate. Both these books post-date *The Neverending Story* (1979) by Michael Ende, in which a bullied schoolboy finds a book titled *The Neverending Story* in a bookshop, and uses it to gain access to the world of Fantastica. Here, books are a troubling portal between worlds. Other children's books are much franker about such claims. A picture book called *Wizardology* (2005) is less a book than a kind of toybox, promising a crystal ball, a wish, and a magic pendant that will allow the child-wearer to find dragons.[21] But as any child will tell you, none of it *really* works.

Books that contain spells actually quoted and used by the child characters offer a particularly attractive promise of access to real magic. They act like recipe books. Anyone with access to the ingredients can try the spell, and often this is what the child-protagonist does. Usually, however, there is one unobtainable ingredient, so the child reader cannot empirically test the magic for him- or herself. In *Carbonel* (1955), the children steal a witch's spellbook in order to release the witch's cat: 'From inside [his jacket] he took out a battered, ancient-looking book. Only one of its powdery leather covers was there, and that hung by a single strand of thread. The pages were thick and yellow, and covered with cramped writing and curious diagrams in red and black ink.'[22] The book is largely useful as a way of undoing a spell: 'Fill the Cauldron with Seven Pipkins of Puddle Water. When the water comes to the boil she must drop in the Plait of Weeds without delay and ride widdershins seven times round the Boiling Pot.'[23] (Note the unstructured but pseudoarchaic use of capital letters.) This is something a child could try at home, though perhaps it would be more accurate to say a child could *pretend* to do so. Such books are almost always filched from bad magic users. Emma Cobley's magic book in Elizabeth Goudge's *Linnets and Valerians* (1964) is an inverse case, being an evil spellbook: 'It was a notebook with covers of hard marbled board and inside the yellow pages were covered with fine copperplate handwriting. On the flyleaf of the book was written, *Emma Cobley. Her book.*'[24] When Nan reads the book, she is afraid, but then she decides that while the spells in it might be wicked 'ranged against them was the goodness of Uncle Ambrose … and the wholesomeness of the animals'.[25] This could be seen as an account of a child reader frightened by being drawn too far into its world.

In the Harry Potter books, the magic book is made comic by its inclusion on a list of Set Books which all students are required to own.

The author's method is to convert a standard textbook name to a magic book by a bit of word substitution ('Magical Theory by Adalbert Waffling'; 'The Dark Forces: A Guide to Self-Protection *by Quentin Trimble*'): the names here reflect the content of the book; theory by Waffling, dark forces by Trimble (or Tremble?).[26] Magic books are normally unique, but here their multiplication and replication into textbooks make magic books seem both more accessible and more everyday. The books are necessarily brand new, too, and in novels most magic books are old, handed down through the generations. Books are magic because they seem to be magic, as every early modern cunning man knew as he flourished his cheap printed fortune-telling book at his clients; they too were dealing in hope.

Magic books can also impress because, like Harry's textbooks, they impersonate the world of learning. In Jonathan Stroud's *Bartimaeus* books (2003–05), Nathaniel must follow an ambitious educational programme, culminating in an encounter with a formidable library of magic books:

> a broad bookcase filled with volumes of every size and colour, ranging from heavy leather-bound lexicons of great antiquity to battered yellow paperbacks with mystic signs scrawled on the spines. 'This is your reading-matter for the next three years,' his master said, tapping the top of the case. 'By the time you're twelve, you must have familiarized yourself with everything it contains.

The books are written in Middle English, Latin, Czech and Hebrew for the most part, although you'll find some Coptic works on the Egyptian rituals of the dead too.'[27]

Here, languages that are incomprehensible now can be mastered. Languages children are likely to know a few words of do not usually feature (though Jewish children may well know some Hebrew). Latin, perhaps the commonest language of magic in Western Europe, is now so rarely taught in schools that the Latin gibberish of Harry Potter has only rarely been noticed.[28]

13 E. Nesbit, by Thomas White of Lewisham, 1892.

In Edward Eager's *Half Magic* (1954), Susan discovers a library book which personalises itself, becoming a book about her and her friends, with blank pages after the moment when she opens the book. The blank pages can be filled in by the children's wishes, and one of them wishes for exciting fantasy adventures, wizards and dragons, in which all of them are caught up; the fantasy takes on the prestige of the ancient magic book. In John Stephens's *The Emerald Atlas* (2010), two children at an orphanage find an old leather book. The alert reader will understand immediately that its age and its parchment pages mean it is ancient (though a bibliographer will wince, and argue that ancient Egyptian books are papyrus, not parchment, and not in leather bindings). The book is not the eponymous atlas, but a machine for turning any photo into a means of time travel. It is described in tactile terms: Kate 'turned another page and touched her fingers to the parchment. She saw a vast army marching along a road, the dust rising from their sandals.'[29]

Sometimes picture books also contain powerful magic books, of which the funniest and cleverest is Art Spiegelman's book *Open Me! I'm a Dog!* (1997). The dog was once a man now transformed, first into a dog, and then into a book shaped like a dog, a book with its own lead. In Vivian French's *The Snow Dragon* (2000) there is a book 'so special that it was always known simply as Book', which requires an orphan child to activate it, whereupon it launches him on a quest for the Snow Dragon; however, the whole story takes place inside the book itself.[30] In E. Nesbit's *The Book of*

14 Thirteenth-century image of a griffon, a beast with a lion's body and the wings and head of an eagle. Here it is carrying off a horse. Bestiaries like this one may have inspired E. Nesbit.

Oxford, Bodleian Library, MS. Bodl. 764, fol. 11v.

Beasts (1900), Lionel inherits a kingdom and a vast library, which includes a volume titled *The Book of Beasts* (*figure* 14). As Lionel turns the pages, the animals in the pictures are liberated:

> The King had turned the next page and there was a shining bird complete and beautiful in every blue feather of him. Under him was written 'Blue Bird of Paradise', and while the King gazed enchanted at the charming picture the Blue Bird fluttered his wings on the yellow page and spread them and flew out of the book.[31]

Lionel releases a dragon from the book and then a hippogriff, a beautiful white horse with swans' wings, which he uses to force the dragon back into the book. Like the magical artefacts in Nesbit's worlds, *The Book of Beasts* is unpredictable. It is not that magic has a price, as it does for Le Guin and Cooper; instead, magic is difficult and unreliable, like people themselves.

A sense that magic may not go according to plan, or might be a portal for a hostile power, may explain why most children's authors seem reluctant to draw on real books of magic. I would like to end with an unusual case of an author who does draw on medieval and early modern grimoires. In Alan Garner's novel *The Moon of Gomrath* (1963), he painstakingly gives sources for his spells (*figure 16*):

> The spells, and many others, are in magical manuscripts at:
> *British Museum*: Sloane 213, 3826, 3853, 2731, 3648, 3884, 3850.
> *Bodleian*: Bod. MS. Rawl. D.253; MS. Bod. e. Mus. 243; Ms. Bod.
>   Rawl. D252; Bod. MS. Ashmole 1406.[32]

Yet, ironically, given Garner's very extensive knowledge of and bookish citation of medieval and early modern magic books, *The Moon of Gomrath* does not feature any magical book as part of the novel. Susan, the child protagonist, reads magic words off the magic bracelet she has been given, and is then inspired to speak further words. Her foe, the Morrigan, knows the spells and magic words by heart. This evasion is in keeping with Garner's discomfort with book magic and Enlightenment learning. For him, book learning has ousted the instinctual native, wild and Celtic

15 (*opposite, top*) Magic symbol from Garner's manuscript of *The Moon of Gomrath*.

Oxford, Bodleian Library, Alan Garner Collection (BYU), Box 7, folder 5, p. 147. © Alan Garner.

16 (*opposite, bottom*) A page of the manuscript of Alan Garner's *Moon of Gomrath*.

Oxford, Bodleian Library, Alan Garner Collection (BYU), Box 7, folder 5, p. 173. © Alan Garner.

17 (*overleaf*) A fifteenth-century collection of texts on magic and fortune telling. The manuscript is referenced by Garner in his note to *The Moon of Gomrath*.

Oxford, Bodleian Library, MS. Rawl. D. 252, fols. 28v–29r.

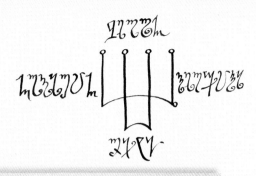

NOTE.

These remaining pages have little to do with the story, and except for a wish to acknowledge many debts, nothing would please me more than that they should stay unread. But so many people have shown an interest in the background of the book that some kind of appendix may be justified.

Firstly, every thing and place mentioned does exist, although I have juggled with one or two local names, and as for Fundindelve, nobody has yet proved that it is not there.

The ingredients of the story are true, or as true as I can make them. The spells are genuine (though incomplete: just in case), and the names are real, even where the characters are invented. A made-up name feels wrong, & When a name is concocted it sounds wrong, but then the problem is to find something authentic that is free from other associations. Boot but Luckily, in Celtic literature there are frequent catalogues of names, people who which may have been the subject of whole cycles of stories, but these are now lost. is possible to find son names that are authentic, lost, & here it yet free from other associations.

Most of the elements and entities in the book are to be seen, in one shape or another, in traditional folk lore. All I have done is to adapt them to my own view.

For example:- The Einheriar were the bodyguard of the gods in Scandanavian mythology, the Herlathing was the English form of the Wild Hunt, and Garanhir, 'the Stalking Person', one of the many names of its leader. (Herne, King Herla, Wild Edric, Gabriel, and magic he prizes: 'The Old Magic is moon magic and sun magic, and it is blood magic, also, and there lie the Hunter's power and his need. He is from a cruel day of the world. Men have changed since they honoured him.'[33] The speaker here, Albanac, explains that the wizards tried to destroy the Old Magic, and that they failed so that 'it would not be destroyed; it would only sleep'. This preverbal magic is meshed with the highest magic in the Western tradition in the spells uttered by both Susan and the Morrigan in their magical duel. The first identifiable spell words come from the *Lesser Book of Honorius*: '*per sedem Baldarey et per gratiam et diligentiam tuam habuisti ab eo hanc nalatimanamilam,* as I command thee.'[34] Garner misspells the name of God, as 'Baldery' instead of Baldarey.[35] This is probably intentional, as he knows that the names *are* the magic in high Western magical traditions. The second spell in the text is also from the tradition of high Western magic:

> *Besticitium consolatio veni ad me vertat Creon, Creon, Creon cantor laudem omnipotentis et non commentur.* [Garner breaks off here] *Stat superior carta bient laudem omviestra principiem da montem et inimicos meos o prostantis vobis et mihi dantes que passium fieri sincisibus.*

Attractively, this spell promises to conjure three ladies to your chamber. This is not real Latin at all, but gibberish.[36] Since all these errors are repeated in *The Moon of Gomrath*, it may be that the spell here is workable *because* it is gibberish, that Garner

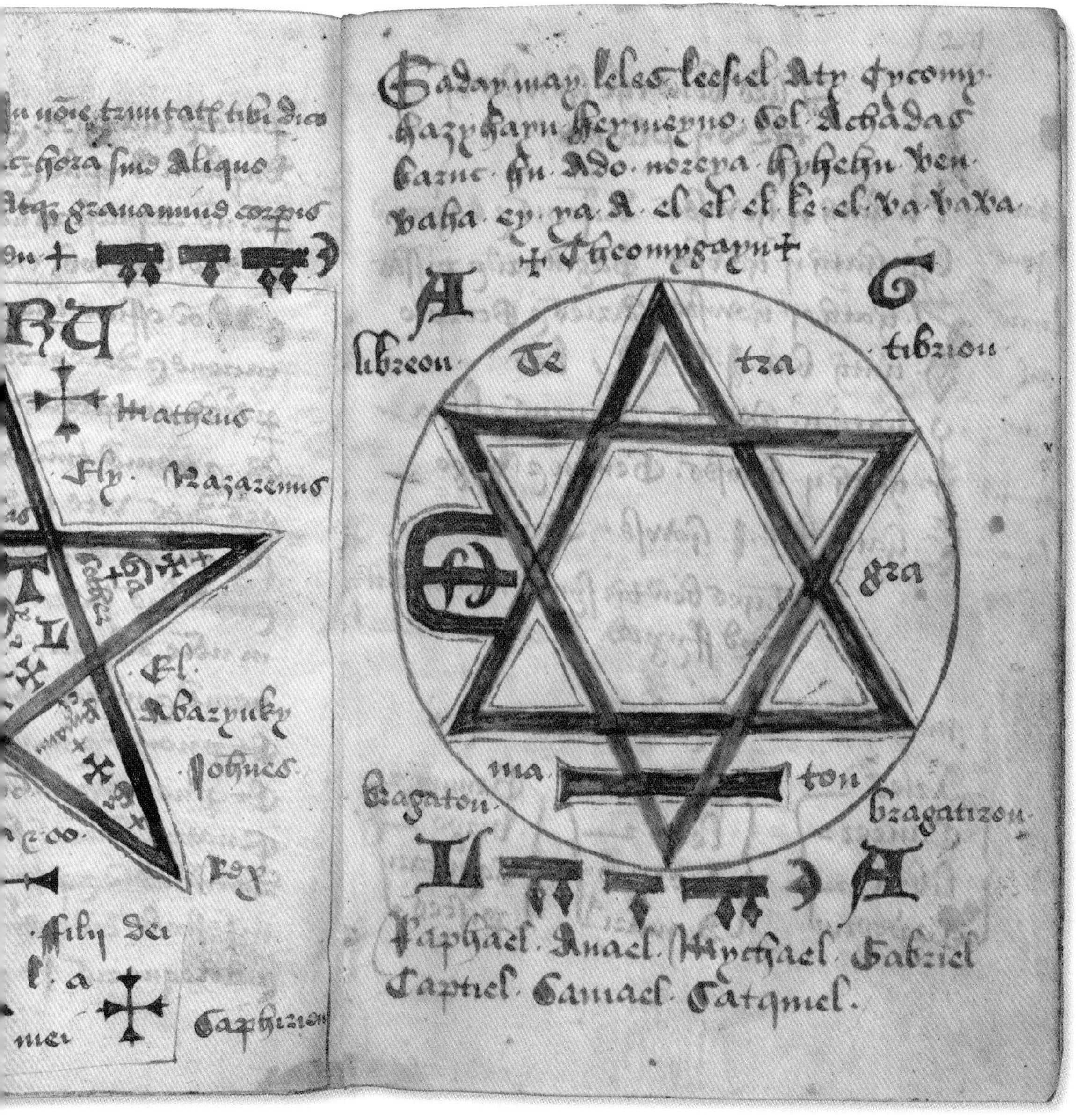

Gadaymay leleo leefief Aty ꝑcomp-
hazyharu Heymeyno. ꞇol Achadaꞇ
barne. Hu Ado. noreya hyhehu ven
vaha. ey ya A. el et et le. el va vaha
+ Hycomygayn+

A ꞇ
hreon   Te   tra   tibriou

Ꝗagaton   ma   ton   bzagatizou

Ꝗaphael. Anael. Mychael. Gabriel.
Captiel. Camael. Catquiel.

libreon
el
el
tra
gra

and . euer . heareafter . at . all . time . and . times,
howers . dayes . nightes . mynittes . and . in . and .
all . places . wheresoeuer . either . in field . hous
or . in . any . other . place . whatsoeuer . & wheresoe
J . shall . call . vpon . thee . and . that . thou .
Elaby : Gathen : doe . not . start . dept . or des
to . goe . or . departe . from . me . neyther . by
arte . or . call . of . any . other . Artist . of an
degree . or Learninge . Whatsoeuer . but . that .
thou . in . the . humblyest . mynd . that . thou .
mayest . be . Comaunded . to attend . and . g
thy . true . obedience . vnto . me . E . A . a
that . euen . as . thou . wilt . Answer . it . v,
and . before . the . Lord . of . hoste . at . the dr
dfull . day . of . Judgment . before . whose . glo
rious . presence . both . thou . and . J . and . all
other . Christian . Creatures . must . and . sh
appeare . to receiue . our . Joyes . in . heauen
or . by . his . doome . to . be . Judged . into . euer

stinge . Damnation . euen . into . the . deepe
pitt . of . hell . there . to . receiue . our port
amoungst . the . diuell . and . his . Angells . to .
euer . burninge . in . pitch . fier . and . brimst

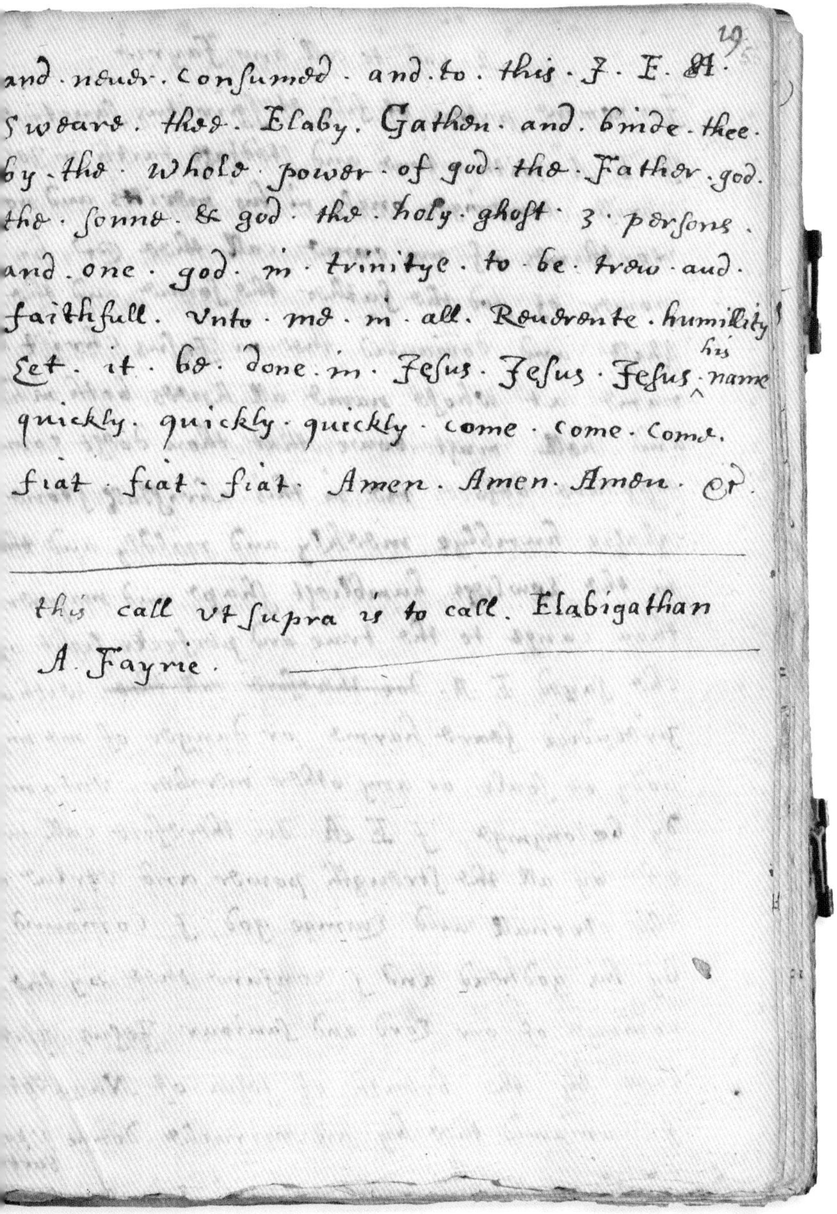

and . neuer . consumed . and . to . this . I . E . A .
sweare . thee . Elaby . Gathen . and . binde . thee .
by . the . whole . power . of god . the . Father . god .
the . sonne . & god . the . holy . ghost . 3 . persons .
and . one . god . in . trinitye . to . be . trew . and .
faithfull . vnto . me . in . all . Reuerente . humility
set . it . be . done . in . Jesus . Jesus . Jesus . name
^his
quickly . quickly . quickly . come . come . come .
fiat . fiat . fiat . Amen . Amen . Amen . &

this call vt supra is to call . Elabigathan
A . Fayrie .

18 An early
seventeenth-century
handbook of
necromancy used by
Garner for *The Moon
of Gomrath*.

Oxford, Bodleian Library,
MS. Ashmole 1406, Part I,
fols. 52v–53r.

is actively exploiting the collapse of language into a stream of unknown and untranslatable sound.

These spells are ritual magic. Usually, in the high magic described in Renaissance texts, ritual magic involves a complex summoning rite in which spirits – demonic or angelic – are conjured. Demonic magic is textually distinguished by its end, which is usually malign, but calls on 'good' entities – angels, saints, God – as in part I of MS. Ashmole 1406, an unusually demonic and even necromantic magic manual (*figure* 18). Texts such as the *Sworn Book of Honorius* and the *Key of Solomon* offer to make the magician closer to and more like the angels, magic as a way of spiritual advancement through prayer and contact with higher planes of being. Such books promise the kind of transcendence that fantasy literature offers its child-protagonists. The Morrigan's final spell makes use of the words '*Fiat! Fiat! Fiat!*' – let it be, let it be, let it be. Garner probably found this in MS. Ashmole 1406: 'Quickly quickly quickly. come come come. Fiat fiat fiat. Amen Amen Amen.'[37]

MS. e Mus. 243 (*figure* 19) is far more benign, containing charms in both Latin and English, some dating from the medieval period, and for the most part a copy of the spells and charms in MS. e Mus. 173. MS. e Mus. 243 is tiny, only 3.4 inches by 2.5 inches, clearly and distinctly written, and organised around the church calendar.[38] It was probably a householder's or cunning person's aide-memoire; it is truly popular magic. Oddly, children's fantasy fiction might be becoming the last resting place of desires and knowledges that were once universal. All magic books, whether 'real' or fictional, offer the power to take us away from the realities of dullness and into delight.

Of the authors discussed here, only C.S. Lewis and Alan Garner, then, make reference to early modern spellbooks. It is

19 A tiny early modern spellbook, 1622.

Oxford, Bodleian Library, MS. e Mus. 243.

scarcely surprising that this is so. The Renaissance grimoire does not have a continuous presence in history, in part because few authors have access to the arcana of great libraries such as the British Library and the Bodleian, with their repositories of the magical books of the past, mostly now forgotten. The magic book therefore has no continuous history, in part because of first Christian and then Enlightenment disdain. Most children's authors therefore do not include the motif of the magic book in their works because they have spent hours poring over medieval spellbooks, but because for them it represents the power of all books to transform and transport their readers. Yet the magic book is also the dark underside of the learning that all books represent, and some children's authors also use it to show troubling power grabs and revolutions.

2

The myths of the north in children's books

CAROLYNE LARRINGTON

The Days of the Week

ODIN with his one piercing eye, shaded by his broad-brimmed hat; red-bearded Thor with his mighty hammer Mjöllnir; grave, beautiful Frigg; untrustworthy yet charming Loki; the brave dragon-fighting hero Sigurd; and the implacable valkyrie Brynhild – these and other Norse gods and heroes became a staple of children's storytelling during the nineteenth century. Annie Keary and her sister Eliza's *The Heroes of Asgard and the Giants of Jötunheim; or, The Week and Its Story* (1857) was the first retelling of Norse myths for children; revised versions would continue to be reprinted well into the twentieth century. First framed as a Christmas-week entertainment for a lively group of children staying at their grandmother's house, *The Heroes of Asgard* opens with the bored youngsters interrupting their aunts and uncles in the library. Aunt Helen is making a drawing of a mysterious tree rising up into the heavens with a serpent twining around its roots and with the rainbow bridge clearly visible. Aunt Helen explains, 'I am drawing a map of the world as our Saxon ancestors supposed it to be, and Uncle Alick is giving me instructions out of that dusty old book.' 'A map of the world!' exclaims the irrepressible Harry, 'Why it is more like a green table than anything else, or a monstrous soup-plate.'[1] Yet the children are intrigued by the picture and the mythological system it represents, and very soon the uncles and aunts have embarked on a project of retelling the myths of the two tribes of Norse gods, the Æsir and Vanir, the giants and dwarves, from Creation to Ragnarök, the end of the world. The tale-telling is organised by the days of the week, the sequence starting with Wednesday, Odin's day, and continuing (Sunday, the Lord's Day, is omitted of course) until the next Wednesday: Christmas Eve. The gods' spectacular fall at Ragnarök thus makes way for the birth of Christ in the Bethlehem stable. *The Heroes of Asgard* is somewhat moralising in its interpretation of the myths: Aunts Helen and Margaret view Loki as the incarnation of evil, for example, while Uncle Alick takes a more advanced view of the mythology, arguing that many tales should be read as nature myth. Thus Loki's betrayal of Baldur represents the forces of winter overcoming summer. The illustrations for this edition are charming if somewhat ahistorical: Freyja visits Ironwood in search of her lost husband while dressed in something like a tutu (*figure*. 2.1).

The first edition of *The Heroes of Asgard* tapped into the growing interest in mid-Victorian Britain in the country's own could tell her where he was gone, and at last her chariot rolled eastward and northward to the very borders of Jötunheim. There Freyja stopped; for before her lay Jarnvid, the Iron Wood, which was one road from earth to the abode of the giants, and whose tall trees, black and hard, were trying to pull down the sky with their iron claws. In the entrance sat an Iron Witch, with her back to the forest and her face towards the Vana. Jarnvid was full of the sons and daughters of this Iron Witch; they were wolves, and bears, and foxes, and many-headed ravenous birds.

"Eastward," croaked a raven as Freyja drew near—

"Eastward in the Iron Wood
The old one sitteth;"

and there she did sit, talking in quarrelsome tones to her wolf-sons and vulture-daughters, who answered from the wood behind her, howling, screeching, and screaming all at the same time. There was a horrible din, and Freyja began to fear that her low voice would never be heard. She was

FREYJA AT THE ENTRANCE OF THE IRON WOOD.

Page 151.

20 Freyja, in distinctly unhistorical clothing, searching for her lost husband Odur, visits the crone of Ironwood. Annie Keary, *The Heroes of Asgard*, 1857.

Oxford, Bodleian Library, 249 u.88.

past. Greek and Roman culture – the *Iliad*, the *Æneid* and Caesar's *The Gallic Wars* – was central to the education of public-school-educated boys. Little wonder, then, that Harry groans at the idea of hearing about gods and heroes, 'Mythology has rather a school sound', until cousin William reminds him 'But we never hear anything about Northern Mythology at school': this is a very different set of divinities.[2] From the mid-eighteenth century

VAFÞRÚÞNISMÁL.

Óþinn kvaþ:

1. 'Ráþ mér nú, Frigg!   alls mik fara tíþir
at vitja Vafþrúþnis;
forvitni mikla   kveþk mér á fornum stöfum
viþ enn alsvinna jötun.'

Frigg kvap:

2. 'Heima letja   mundak Herjaföþr
í görþum goþa;
þvít engi jötun   hugþak jafnramman
sem Vafþrúþni vesa.'

Vafþráþnismál.—*In* **R,** *No. 3, st. 20 to the end in* **A,** *cited in* **Sn. E.**

THE WORDS OF THE MIGHTY WEAVER.

Odin.

1. Now counsel me, Frigg   for I fain would seek
the Mighty Weaver of words.
I yearn to strive   with that all-wise giant
in learning of olden lore.

Frigg.

2. Nay, Father of Hosts!   I fain would keep thee
at home in the garth of the gods;
no giant I deem   so dread and wise
as that Mighty Weaver of words.

onwards, British writers had begun to reach back into the pre-Conquest past of the islands, seeking subjects from a period when Englishness (with a Viking admixture) and Celticness were clearly identifiable, kindling interest in 'the beauty and grandeur of the old tales in which our forefathers believed', as Uncle Alick puts it. This fascination with the early medieval past coincided with the rediscovery of early texts, now newly edited and translated. Annie Keary's source, 'that dusty old book' as disrespectful Harry calls

21 The Elder or Poetic Edda, translated by Olive Bray, 1908. On the verso, Vidar avenging the death of his father Odin on the wolf Fenrir; on the recto, Odin places Baldur on the funeral pyre. Illustrations by W.G. Collingwood.

Oxford, Bodleian Library, Soc. 27858 e.12, pp. 38–9.

22 Odin and his Ravens, Hugin and Munin, *Kongesagaer*, ed. Gustav Storm, (Kristiania, Stenersen, 1899). Illustrations by Gerhard Munthe.

Oxford, English Faculty Library, A.2.7.5, p. 54.

it, was Bishop Percy's *Northern Antiquities* of 1770, a translation of Paul Henri's Mallet's two volumes, *Introduction à l'historie de Dannemarc* and *Monumens de la mythologie et de la poésie des Celtes*, published in 1755 and 1766 respectively. Mallet relied on recently published Danish versions of the two crucial texts for understanding Old Norse myth: the Poetic Edda and the Prose Edda. The first of these is a collection of mythological and heroic poems, written down in Iceland around 1270, but originating in much earlier oral tradition. The Prose Edda was written around 1220 by the Icelandic politician and scholar Snorri Sturluson; composing a manual for would-be poets, he found it necessary to explain the mythological allusions in traditional Norse poetic forms and so he produced a systematic account of Norse myth from Creation to Ragnarök. With facing Latin translations, the eighteenth-century editions of these two works made it possible for those with little or no knowledge of Old Norse to make new versions of the myths for different audiences (*figures* 21 & 22).

Strid. Der faldt Haakon Jarl, men Atle Jarl blev dødelig saaret, og fór de met til Atleø[3], og der døde han. Saa siger Øivind Skaldespilder:

Blev Haakon,
Hærmanden,
fældet, da han
fór til Kamp,
og sit Liv
i Oddenes Leg
Frøis Ætling
paa Fjaler endte.

Og der, hvor segnede
Grjotgards Søns
Venneskarer,
Vaagen om Stavenes
blandet blev
med Blod af Mænd
i Strids-gudens
store Gny.

A second edition of *Northern Antiquities* with a translation of the Prose Edda was issued in 1847. The new version has a splendid frontispiece illustrating the Norse conception of the world: this is what Aunt Helen is copying in the library (*figure 23*). Later editions of *The Heroes of Asgard* took account of new scholarly work, including Benjamin Thorpe's 1860 translation of the Poetic Edda and German scholarship which drew on the pioneering comparative work of the Grimm brothers. These subsequent versions, now with Annie's sister Eliza named as author, drop the days-of-the-week framework and the two generations of storytellers and listeners vanish. Yet this format turns out still to be useful in one

23 The World-Tree Yggdrasill, 'The Mundane Tree', and the Norse Cosmos. Frontispiece of *Northern Antiquities*, translated from the French of M. Mallet by Bishop Percy. (Second edition, 1847).

NORTHERN ANTIQUITIES;

OR,

AN HISTORICAL ACCOUNT OF THE MANNERS, CUSTOMS, RELIGION AND LAWS, MARITIME EXPEDITIONS AND DISCOVERIES, LANGUAGE AND LITERATURE

OF THE

ANCIENT SCANDINAVIANS,

(DANES, SWEDES, NORWEGIANS AND ICELANDERS.)

WITH INCIDENTAL NOTICES RESPECTING OUR SAXON ANCESTORS.

TRANSLATED FROM THE FRENCH OF M. MALLET,

BY BISHOP PERCY.

NEW EDITION,

REVISED THROUGHOUT, AND CONSIDERABLY ENLARGED; WITH A TRANSLATION OF THE PROSE EDDA FROM THE ORIGINAL OLD NORSE TEXT; AND NOTES CRITICAL AND EXPLANATORY,

BY I. A. BLACKWELL, ESQ.

TO WHICH IS ADDED,

AN ABSTRACT OF THE EYRBYGGJA SAGA.

By Sir Walter Scott.

LONDON.
HENRY G. BOHN, YORK STREET, COVENT GARDEN.
1847.

YGGDRASILL,

The Mundane Tree.

24 Mr Wedding (Odin) and his raven from Diana Wynne Jones, *Eight Days of Luke.*

HarperCollins, 2011, p. 95.
Illustrated by David Wyatt.
© David Wyatt.

of the first important twentieth-century re-imaginings of Norse mythic characters: Diana Wynne Jones's lively and funny *Eight Days of Luke* (1975). In this novel lonely young David accidentally releases Loki (Luke), manifested as a charming and untruthful boy of his own age, from his chains. Mr Wedding (Odin) Mr Chew (Tyr or Tiw) and Mr and Mrs Fry (Freyr and Freyja) all appear in the neighbourhood, and they browbeat young Luke just as badly as David's bullying family treat him. David notices 'how small and frightened Luke's harassed figure looked among them. Never had David felt for anyone more. It was just like himself among his own relations.'[3] The gods are seeking Thor's hammer, stolen by Sigurd and Brunhilda. Mr Wedding nicely retains Odin's wisdom, fierceness and plausibility (*figure 24*). He strikes a bargain with David that Luke will remain free if David can recover the hammer;

in this quest David learns to stand up for himself and is freed from his dreadful relatives. Though the hammer is recovered, not all breaches are healed: 'It came home to David that Luke and Mr Wedding were going to be on opposites sides, when that final battle came.'[4]

Dr Wägner (and A.S. Byatt)

The learned tone of the new Introduction to *The Heroes of Asgard*'s second edition was echoed in another influential nineteenth-century retelling of the myths, *Asgard and the Gods*. Translating a German work by Dr Wilhelm Wägner, it was published in London and New York in 1880, and regularly reprinted until 1917 (*figure 25*). Wägner incorporates the latest thinking about Norse myth in relation to German history, legend and folklore, and the emerging discipline of comparative mythology. Thus the book often refers to battles between Good and Evil in Sanskrit and Persian mythologies, and full explanations about the origins of the gods' names as currently understood. Fertility myth is the dominant mode of explanation: the tale of Freyr and Gerdr, in which the god sends his servant Skirnir to woo the giant maiden Gerdr with a combination of gifts, bribes and

finally the threat of a terrifying curse, is interpreted as summer overcoming winter: the forces of fertility must break down the resistance of the frost-bound earth and awaken her to new life and growth. Loki's prank in cutting off the hair of Thor's wife Sif is interpreted thus: 'Sif's hair is that of the earth goddess, the flowers and corn which grow upon the earth. The winter-demon robs her of her hair and leaves her head quite bald.'[5] Not all the allegorical interpretations which Wägner proposes are rooted in seasonal cycles; the story of Thor's failure in his expedition to visit the giant Utgarda-Loki shows that 'not even the mighty Ase could make it possible to cultivate the mountains.'[6] The comic tale of Thor's loss of his hammer, in which he must dress in women's clothing and present himself as the bride of Thrym, the giant who has stolen it, is about land clearance; once the disguised Thor has recovered his hammer and smashed all the giants into smithereens, humans can cultivate the land he has opened up for them.

Wägner's style, as mediated by his translator, is wonderfully grand: 'Men, longing for knowledge, and loving the history of old Germany, sought for the great goddess Saga with untiring diligence, until at length they found her. She dwelt in a house of crystal beneath the cool flowing river.'[7] Stories are interspersed with commentary, and the story of creation and the origin of the gods is related in the present tense at a swift and exciting pace. Wägner adds some folktales into his account, expanding the limited eddic myths with an unusual tale from the Faeroe Islands. This unusually depicts Loki as kindly and helpful to humans, aiding a peasant family to fight off the depredations of the giant Skrimsli. The tale of the origin of flax (a gift from Frigg) also makes its first appearance here; these folk tales would persist in later Norse myth collections right up to the 1980s.

Norse myth, notes Wägner, has 'many unlovely and even coarse ideas … mixed up with the rest and … they cannot be compared with the beautiful fancies of Hellenic poetry; but the drama as a whole is grand and philosophical'.[8] Norse myth was nevertheless easier to make wholesome for young people than the Greek mythic heritage. In contrast to the adulteries of Zeus, only Odin begets children out of wedlock; this can be explained as occurring before his marriage to Frigg or in response to the prophecies surrounding the death of Baldr. The suspicion of incest between Njörd, father of Freyr and Freyja, and his sister is omitted, and the remaining tales with sexual or scatalogical elements are easily bowdlerised. Thus Freyja, according to the Kearys, persuades the dwarves to give her the *Brisinga men* necklace by sheer charm, rather than by sleeping with each in turn. Children are also spared the spectacle of Loki tying a goat by the beard to his testicles in order to make the giantess Skadi laugh, when she comes to Asgard bent on revenge for her father Thjazi.

The religion of the Æsir endowed the German ancestors with 'strength and courage enough to shatter the might of the Roman Empire', boasts Wägner, referring to Arminius's victory over the Roman legions at the Battle of the Teutoburg Forest in 9 CE.[9] Although this triumph has less resonance for British readers,

Wägner's translator rightly assumes a close kinship between the English and the Germans in the nineteenth century: both nations were Germanic in origin, defining themselves against the excitable southern Europeans, and sharing virtues such as a strong work ethic, common sense, and a romantic love of rugged, dramatic Nature. Wägner's work begot an unexpected sequel, for it was a treasured childhood book of A.S. Byatt. In 2011 she published *Ragnarok*, her reflections on her reading of these strongly German-inflected myths in the context of the Second World War when her father was away fighting, and who would, she thought, like Baldr, never return.[10] Sixty-five years later, Byatt re-reads the book which so strongly shaped her northern identity and pessimistic imagination, producing a complex meditation on memory, the natural world and environmental collapse.

Heroic legend: Morris and Wagner

Heroic legends from the Eddas are trickier to adapt for children than the exploits of the gods. The tale of Sigurd the Dragon-Slayer became popular after William Morris composed *Sigurd the Volsung* in 1876, the year of the first performance of Richard Wagner's Ring Cycle.[11] Though Morris did not care for Wagner – 'the idea of a sandy haired German tenor tweedledeeing over the unspeakable woes of Sigurd' was more than he could bear, his biographer notes – he felt that the story of the Volsungs was 'the Great Story of the North, which should be to all our race what the Tale of Troy was

26 William Morris's epic poem *Sigurd the Volsung*. Frontispiece, 1876.

Oxford, Bodleian Library, Kelmscott Press c.1.

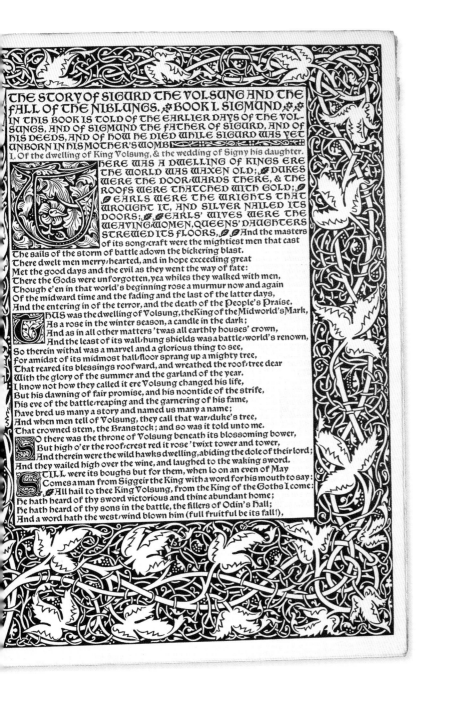

THE STORY OF SIGURD THE VOLSUNG AND THE FALL OF THE NIBLUNGS. ❧ BOOK I. SIGMUND ❧

IN THIS BOOK IS TOLD OF THE EARLIER DAYS OF THE VOLSUNGS, AND OF SIGMUND THE FATHER OF SIGURD, AND OF HIS DEEDS, AND OF HOW HE DIED WHILE SIGURD WAS YET UNBORN IN HIS MOTHER'S WOMB.

I. Of the dwelling of King Volsung, & the wedding of Signy his daughter.

THERE WAS A DWELLING OF KINGS ERE THE WORLD WAS WAXEN OLD; ❧ DUKES WERE THE DOOR-WARDS THERE, & THE ROOFS WERE THATCHED WITH GOLD; ❧ EARLS WERE THE WRIGHTS THAT WROUGHT IT, AND SILVER NAILED ITS DOORS; ❧ EARLS' WIVES WERE THE WEAVING-WOMEN, QUEENS' DAUGHTERS STREWED ITS FLOORS, ❧ And the masters of its song-craft were the mightiest men that cast
The sails of the storm of battle adown the bickering blast.
There dwelt men merry-hearted, and in hope exceeding great
Met the good days and the evil as they went the way of fate:
There the Gods were unforgotten, yea whiles they walked with men,
Though e'en in that world's beginning rose a murmur now and again
Of the midward time and the fading and the last of the latter days,
And the entering in of the terror, and the death of the People's Praise.

THUS was the dwelling of Volsung, the King of the Midworld's Mark,
As a rose in the winter season, a candle in the dark;
And as in all other matters 'twas all earthly houses' crown,
And the least of its wall-hung shields was a battle-world's renown,
So therein withal was a marvel and a glorious thing to see,
For amidst of its midmost hall-floor sprang up a mighty tree,
That reared its blessings roofward, and wreathed the roof-tree dear
With the glory of the summer and the garland of the year.
I know not how they called it ere Volsung changed his life,
But his dawning of fair promise, and his noontide of the strife,
His eve of the battle-reaping and the garnering of his fame,
Have bred us many a story and named us many a name;
And when men tell of Volsung, they call that war-duke's tree,
That crowned stem, the Branstock; and so was it told unto me.

SO there was the throne of Volsung beneath its blossoming bower,
But high o'er the roof-crest red it rose 'twixt tower and tower,
And therein were the wild hawks dwelling, abiding the dole of their lord;
And they wailed high over the wine, and laughed to the waking sword.

STILL were its boughs but for them, when lo on an even of May
Comes a man from Siggeir the King with a word for his mouth to say:
❧ All hail to thee King Volsung, from the King of the Goths I come:
He hath heard of thy sword victorious and thine abundant home;
He hath heard of thy sons in the battle, the fillers of Odin's Hall;
And a word hath the west-wind blown him (full fruitful be its fall!),

to the Greeks' (*figure* 26).[12] Morris's poem received mixed notices initially, but the story of Sigurd's triumphs over his scheming foster-father and the dragon Fafnir, his downfall through the treachery of his brothers-in-law, his complex and anguished relationships with Brynhild and with his wife Gudrun had become a school textbook by 1905, though large stretches of Morris's expansive, hypnotic poetry had been replaced by prose summaries.[13]

Wagner's Ring Cycle became central to popular understanding of Norse legend after its premiere in London in 1882; his *Die Walküre*, *Siegfried* and *Götterdämmerung* cover the same ground as Morris's poem, though of course the latter does not end in Ragnarök. Translations of the Ring libretto into English by Margaret Armour were published in 1910 and 1911 (*figure* 27) with illustrations by Arthur Rackham; the association of the artist who had illustrated Grimms' Fairy Tales and other works for children doubtless encouraged young people to look at the books.[14] C.S. Lewis's passion for 'pure "Northernness" … a vision of huge, clear spaces hanging above the Atlantic in the endless twilight of Northern summer, remoteness, severity' was triggered by reading the Christmas supplement of *The Bookman* for 1911, which contained a colour illustration from the newly published libretto for *Siegfried* and *Götterdämmerung*, depicting Siegfried and the Rhinemaidens (*see figure* 7).[15] After seeing the fifteen-guinea de luxe edition at a cousin's house, Lewis soon persuaded his brother to go halves on buying the cheaper version, and would ask for the first Armour and Rackham volume for his birthday the following year. 'Of course a

27 Siegfried licks
Fafner's blood from his
finger, thus learning
to understand the
language of birds and
that his foster-father
intends to murder him.
Arthur Rackham's
illustration to Margaret
Armour's translation
of Wagner's *Siegfried*,
1910.

Oxford, Bodleian Library,
Castello 31, illustration
opposite p. 58.

great deal of my pleasure in it [the libretto of Siegfried] is owing to Rackham's pictures: still it is lovely wild poetry', he wrote to his friend Arthur Greeves in 1917.[16] Lewis's enthusiasm for the north continued to inflect his writing – the eternal wintriness of *The Lion, the Witch and the Wardrobe* and the evil wolves of Narnia recall the Norse *fimbulvetr* (mighty winter) and the ravening wolves who pervade Ragnarök.[17] Norse influences are less obvious in the rest of the series, yet, as Lewis later wrote to a reviewer of his adult novel *That Hideous Strength* (1945), they persisted in his imagination, 'You just missed tapping my whole Norse complex – Old Icelandic, Wagner's *Ring* and (again) Morris.'[18]

Wagner's Ring Cycle thus increased interest in Norse heroic legend in the early twentieth century. Although J.R.R. Tolkien would protest that the only connection between his epic *The Lord of the Rings* and the opera cycle was that 'both rings were round, and there the resemblance ceased', he and Lewis could be found in 1934 reading out loud Wagner's libretto to *Die Walküre* in the original German while Lewis's brother Warnie followed along with an English translation.[19] 'Arising out of the perplexities of Wotan we had a long and interesting discussion on religion', Warnie noted in his diary.[20]

Tolkien and the Nazis

As Professor of Anglo-Saxon at Oxford, Tolkien also taught and studied Norse poems and sagas. He had made detailed use of

Norse heroic legend, in particular *Völsunga saga*, Wagner's major source, in the early unfinished story *The Children of Hurin*, begun in the form of an epic poem during the First World War. The tale was finally completed by Christopher Tolkien and published in 2007.[21] Here Tolkien created the dragon Glaurung, a close ally of Morgoth, as cunning as the great Norse dragon Fafnir, and an evil dwarf called Mîm who betrays the hero Túrin. The themes of brother–sister incest and the reforging of the ancestral sword also appear. When the dying Glaurung reveals the truth about their sibling bond to Niënor, the sister, now married to and pregnant by Túrin, both the Children commit suicide.

Norse myth is less central in *The Lord of the Rings* (1954–55) than is Anglo-Saxon culture, but Tolkien had already exploited the figures and motifs of northern legend in *The Hobbit* (1937).[22] Bilbo the hobbit's journey begins when the wizard Gandalf brings a group of dwarves, whose names are borrowed from the Poetic Edda, to Bilbo's house. They are on a quest to win back the Lonely Mountain from the dragon Smaug and to gain the dragon's treasure; Bilbo is signed up as the band's 'burglar'. En route they meet hulking, stupid trolls, creatures of Norse folklore though speaking pure Cockney, who are eventually turned into stone by the dawn. Bilbo's riddle contest with Gollum takes its inspiration from the Norse saga of King Heidrek, which Tolkien's son Christopher would grow up to edit. Bilbo and Gollum exchange riddles which are closer to the Old English tradition than the Norse riddles offered up by the disguised Odin in the saga. Both Bilbo and

Odin win their contests by asking an unanswerable question which strictly speaking is not a riddle at all. Odin's question: 'What did Odin whisper in his son Baldr's ear on his funeral pyre' can only be answered by the god himself. Bilbo's simple question, 'What have I got in my pocket?' infuriates Gollum in its deviation from the standard riddle form, and he cries, 'Not fair! Not fair!'[23] Yet the trajectory of Tolkien's masterpiece hinges on Gollum's failure to guess the answer: for it is, of course, the Ring.

Travelling through the dark forest of Mirkwood, a mysterious area often traversed by warriors in Eddic heroic poetry, hobbit and dwarves come eventually to the dragon's lair. Although Bilbo's theft of the dragon's cup, Smaug's ability to fly, and his fiery breath stem from the dragon of the Old English poem *Beowulf* (*figure* 28), Smaug's intelligence and capacity for speech align him with the Norse dragon Fafnir. Sigurd engages in a long conversation with this monster after he has dealt Fafnir his death-blow; Bilbo is reconnoitring the dragon's lair when the dragon tries to entice him close enough to attack (*figure* 29). Bilbo flatters him, 'O Smaug, the Chiefest and Greatest of Calamities', and hides his identity in riddles: 'I am the clue-finder, the web-cutter, the stinging fly. I was chosen for the lucky number', for, as Tolkien observes, 'This … is the way to talk to dragons … no dragon can resist the fascination of riddling talk.'[24] Tolkien claimed that the original impetus for *Lord of the Rings* and *The Silmarillion* was 'fundamentally linguistic', and his ingenuity in naming his characters bears witness to his delight in language. Smaug, for example, derives his name from

ꝥÆT ꝥE GARDE
na in geap dagum. þeod cynninga
þrym ge frunon huda æþelingas elle
fre medon. Oft scyld sceffing sceaþe
þreatum monegū mægþum meodo setla
of teah eg sode eorl syððan ærest peaʒ
fea sceaft funden he þæs frofre gebad
peox under polenum peorð myndum þah
oð ꝥ him æghpyle þara ymb sittendra
ofer hron rade hyran scolde gomban
gyldan þpæs god cyning. ðæm eafera pæs
æfter cenned geong in geardum þone god
sende folce to frofre fyren ðearfe on
geat þ hie ær drugon aldor ... ase. lange
hpile him þæs lif frea puldres pealdend
porold are for geaf. beopulf pæs bren e
blæd pide sprang. scyld ... eafera scede
landum in. Spa sce ... ... gode
ge pyrcean ... ...

28 The first leaf of
the eleventh-century
manuscript of *Beowulf*.

London, British Library,
Cotton MS. Vitellius A.
XV. © British Library
Board.

Conversation with Smaug

the past tense of the Old Norse verb *smjúga* 'to creep'; Smeagol (Gollum's original name) comes from the same root, but in the form to which it mutated in Old English.

In the post-war context in which *The Lord of the Rings* was published interest in Norse myths had waned considerably. Nazism had made use of Norse myths and legends as a basis for a nationalist ideology which argued for the superiority of Aryans, those who shared a Germanic heritage, over other races. Hitler himself was irritated by those who wanted to revive the cult of the old gods, but the imagery of, for example, Germany as a sleeping valkyrie, awakened by the hero Hitler–Sigurd became highly potent in Nazi propaganda. Wagner's operas too, so popular with Hitler, who was a regular visitor to the Bayreuth Festival, became tarnished by Nazi associations.[25] Hitler's enthusiasm was not widely shared by the party bosses; 'the colossal anomaly is that just about the only person in the party that liked Wagner's operas was Hitler himself', notes Frederic Spotts.[26] Nor was the Ring Cycle on the programme at Bayreuth after 1942, and in that year only *Götterdämmerung*, in a special performance for the injured from the Russian front, was scheduled.[27]

Post-war retellings

By the time Barbara Leonie Picard wrote *Tales of the Norse Gods and Heroes*, published by Oxford University Press in 1953, it was high time to reclaim Norse myths from the Germanicisation of

Wägner and Wagner. Picard includes the story of the Völsungs, Sigurd's ancestors, and continues after Sigurd's death with the story of his widow Gudrun, forced by her family to marry Atli, the brother of Brynhild (*figure* 30). When Atli murdered her brothers because they refused to disclose the whereabouts of Sigurd's treasure-hoard, won from Fafnir, and which had passed to them on their brother-in-law's death, Gudrun killed her children by Atli, fed their flesh to him and his men as snacks with their beer, then stabbed him in his sleep and set fire to his hall. Picard leaves out the child-killing and cannibalism, lest she traumatise her young readers. Her versions of the stories are direct and unvarnished, if still shaped by nature myth: 'here are the stories of their gods, gods who were even such as every Norseman longed to be: brave, dauntless warriors or cunning tricksters, with their lovely loyal wives, for ever striving against the hated giants who were the pitiless northern snows and frosts, and the grim northern mountains'.[28] Picard's versions spoke directly to children of the 1950s and 1960s: one such reader was Melvin Burgess, whose *Bloodtide* and *Bloodsong* are discussed below.

Roger Lancelyn Green was taught by C.S. Lewis at Merton College, Oxford before the Second World War; after the war he returned to Oxford to write a thesis on the nineteenth-century fairy-tale compiler Andrew Lang under Tolkien's supervision. His greatest success as a writer came with his retellings of tales which he loved as a child, a 'recreative enterprise' as the *Dictionary of National Biography* terms it.[29] *Myths of the Norsemen* (1960), also

30 Sigurd and Brynhild on their shared funeral pyre. Illustration by Joan Kiddell-Munroe from *Tales of the Norse Gods and Heroes* by Barbara Leonie Picard (1953).

Oxford, Bodleian Library, 930 e.853, pp. 272–3. Reproduced by permission of Oxford University Press.

published as *The Saga of Asgard*, was written with scholarly knowledge and vivid language.[30] There are occasional archaic forms, but
Green's writing is lively and direct: memorably he christens the
goats who pull Thor's chariot Gaptooth and Cracktooth and he
sets out a clear trajectory for the stories from Ginnungagap, the
chaos before Creation, to the rebirth of the world after Ragnarök.
Lancelyn Green was friendly with both Lewis and Tolkien; in
his study of C.S. Lewis he recalls how he encouraged the author
to continue his draft of *The Lion, the Witch and the Wardrobe*,

which Tolkien, 'wedded to different modes of thought where fairy tales and fantasy were concerned', had disliked intensely. Lancelyn Green, by contrast, 'perhaps saw more clearly that here was the beginning of a really new and exciting development in children's literature … the land where it was always winter, but never Christmas'.[31]

Kevin Crossley-Holland's *The Norse Myths* (1980), now the *Penguin Book of Norse Myths*, was not orginally aimed at young readers, though its beautiful endpapers with their cosmological plan echo the illustrations of the World Tree in *Northern Antiquities* and the 1857 *Heroes of Asgard*.[32] A selection of the myths for children was published later, however, as *Axe-Age, Wolf-Age* (1985), whose title quotes lines from the Poetic Edda foreshadowing Ragnarök. Crossley-Holland's deep knowledge of both Old English and Old Norse has borne fruit in his most recent book for children, the beautifully written *Bracelet of Bones* (2011). Set in the early eleventh century, when belief in the Norse gods was still living, *Bracelet of Bones* tells of the quest of young Solveig for her father, who has left their farm in a dark Norwegian fjord to join the future king Harald Sigurdsson in far Byzantium, breaking the promise he made to take her with him. Crossley-Holland vividly evokes the tense atmosphere in trading towns such as Birka and Stara Ladoga, where merchants deal in glossy, deep-piled furs, 'hunks of wax, boardgames of draughts and chess, boxes of salt, two wooden platters glistening with honey scooped out of one of the barrels', and the artefacts which Solveig, herself a skilled carver, manages to shape from walrus ivory and other bone.[33] Solveig makes the demanding, perilous journey along the great rivers of Russia, across the Black Sea to the gleaming city of Byzantium and comes to find a substitute family, with enemies and allies, among the ship's crew. In an afterword the author notes that he was inspired by runic graffiti recording the Norse name 'Halfdan', carved high up in Hagia Sophia in Constantinople, a name which he gives to his heroine's father. Other children's authors have set tales of adventure in the Viking age; these are too numerous to discuss here.

The gods in the modern world

Crossley-Holland's decision to make his heroine a fourteen-year-old girl allows him to get away from battles and Viking violence, though other dangers beset Solveig on her quest. Like A.S. Byatt, girls enjoy the tales of the Norse gods, but they find few inspiring role models among the goddesses and valkyries. Freyja seems obsessed with jewellery; Keary even claims that Freyja loses her husband Odur because 'Brisingamen and Odur could not live together in the palace of Folkvang'.[34] Idunn, guardian of the apples of immortality, trustingly believes Loki's tale of finding similar apples out in the forest and is betrayed to the giant Thjazi, while Frigg's attempt to protect her son Baldur from his impending death is futile.

Alan Garner, one of the most influential and popular children's writers of the post-war era, fuses the widespread legend of the sleepers in the cave, localised at Alderley Edge in his native Cheshire, with elements taken from Norse, Anglo-Saxon and, increasingly, Celtic sources in his series comprising *The Weirdstone of Brisingamen* (1960), *The Moon of Gomrath* (1963) and *Boneland* (2012).[35] Garner drew on Norse myth for many of the names of the supernatural beings who move through the Cheshire landscape, some aiding and some hindering the efforts of the wizard Cadellin Silverbrow to recover the lost Weirdstone, the source of the magic which preserves the sleepers in the cave. The silent and powerful elves (the *ljósálfar* or light-elves, borrowed from Snorri Sturluson's *Edda*) are, in *The Moon of Gomrath*, prominent allies of the novels' child-heroes, Colin and Susan. The dwarves are also on the side of good in *The Weirdstone*; these seem to have more in common with Tolkien's re-imagining of Norse dwarves than any marked similarity to the often evil dwarves of Norse myth. Nevertheless the heroic dwarf Durathror, prince of the Huldrafolk (or Hidden

People – an Icelandic designation normally used for elves) bears a Norse-sounding name, and he has the engaging habit of swearing by elements of Norse mythology: 'By the cow of Orgelmir!' 'By the blood of Lodur!', which go unglossed in the text.[36] Durathror has the ability to fly, unusual in dwarves, for he has exchanged the Tarnhelm, or helmet of invisibility, a dwarfish treasure, for Valham, 'falcon-shape', a feather-coat which enables the wearer to fly and which is normally the property of Freyja. Another link with Freyja is the name of the magic stone; although it is usually referred to as 'Firefrost', a paradoxical description of the light which pours from the stone's heart, it is also the 'Weirdstone' (the Stone of Fate) and ascribed to Brisingamen. This name, shared with Freyja's precious necklace gained from the dwarves, which has no particular magic power, is used without explanation by Cadellin and the authorial voice alike.

Names and figures which derive directly from Old Norse are mainly attached to evil characters in *Weirdstone*, such as the *svarts*, the goblin-like Dark Elves who serve evil ends. Elsewhere place names, events and personal names become oddly jumbled in Garner's retelling so that the hellish region of Náströnd (Corpse-beach) from the Poetic Edda becomes the name of a profoundly evil wizard 'the great spirit of darkness' who pits himself against Cadellin and the children. Nastrond lives in the Abyss of Ragnarok, a place rather than the destruction of the world which it signifies in Norse. His main agent in the tale is Grimnir, a shadowy figure who shares a name and some of his characteristics with the god

Odin. The morthbrood (witches and warlocks), led by Grimnir and his associate the Celtic battle-goddess, the Morrigan, with the aid of Rimthur (Frost-Giant), conjure up 'the ice-giant's breath', an intense winter storm – the Fimbulwinter which signals Ragnarök in Norse myth – and one of the cosmic wolves who in the Norse myth of the end-time will swallow the sun and the moon, the mighty Wolf Managarm (Hound of the Moon), is unleashed by Nastrond.

> All the sky to the north and east was wolf head. The mouth yawned wider, till there was nothing to be seen but the black, cavernous maw, rushing down to swallow hill and valley whole.[37]

Although the dying Grimnir, struck down by his brother Cadellin, refuses to break his silence and to acknowledge his brother-double, in the hope that Managarm will prevail, Managarm is finally repelled by Firefrost, once more in Cadellin's hands. Garner employs figures from Nordic folklore too; the *stromkarl*, a musical river-spirit who sings prophetically, and huge, hideous trollwomen, the *mara* (associated with the *-mare* of 'nightmare') stalk across the land. The two children are brave and feisty heroes, and Susan never plays second fiddle to her brother; as the keeper of the stone, she often takes the initiative and plunges into the action where Colin fears to tread. In *The Moon of Gomrath* she fights with sword and shield, and rescues the kidnapped Colin from the Morrigan.

Other Viking Age-set children's books often have adventurous boys as their heroes, but some recent young adult novels, taking their cue perhaps from Susan, find a role for girls where myth, magic and skill, rather than physical strength, are at stake. So Joanne Harris's series *Runemarks* (2007) and *Runelight* (2011) foreground their heroine's understanding of runes. The runic alphabet was used by Germanic peoples before they acquired the Latin alphabet when they converted to Christianity, and the two alphabets continued side-by-side for a long time. Runes may also have had magical functions. Hence Tolkien and certain other children's authors use them for their mysteriousness, their magical affiliations and as a sort of code which readers inside and outside the books must crack.

32 A postcard written in runic to Tolkien by the writer Kay Farrer, 1947, in response to correspondence from him, also in runic. The text for this postcard reads: Dear Professor Tolkien, Thank you for taking my impertinence so kindly. I should prize a key to the Dwarvish alphabet very highly indeed, when you are more at leisure. Yours sincerely Katharine Farrer. Runes also feature on the dust-jacket design for *The Hobbit* (see p. viii).

Oxford, Bodleian Library, MS. Tolkien 21, fol. 56. © The J.R.R. Tolkien Estate Limited 2013.

Runemarks and *Runelight* feature attractive heroines who are, like Solveig, as brave and resourceful as any god.[38] The first novel introduces fourteen-year-old Maddie, who lives in a quasi-medieval world in which magic is possible, if frowned on, and where goblins make a nuisance of themselves in the pub cellar. A no-nonsense northern lass, Maddie is an outcast in the village, bearing a 'ruinmark' which suggests some association with the lost gods. The Æsir disappeared at Ragnarök, after which the Order, an unforgiving and obsessively Book-based religion, has taken control. Maddie finds a mentor, One-Eye the wanderer, who recruits her to recover a mysterious object from the World Below. Maddie's quest revives the gods, not destroyed after all, but rather biding their time in the hope of rebuilding Asgard. Harris puts her knowledge of the myths and of various runic alphabets to good use in *Runemarks* and its sequel. The influence of Philip Pullman's depiction of 'the Authority' in the *His Dark Materials* trilogy can be detected in the religious tyranny of the Order, but Maddie is a bold and fearless heroine and her affection for the untrustworthy, yet charming, Loki is infectious. Some of the other gods – Skadi in wolf-form for example, still nursing a millennia-old grudge against Loki – are depicted with powerful imaginative force: 'a white snow-wolf brindled with grey; dark muzzle folded in a velvet snarl displaying teeth as sharp and white as a row of icicles'.[39] Making use of the whole pantheon of the Æsir and the Vanir proves overambitious: Freyja, whining about her clothes; Idunn, the dippy flower-child; Bragi, constantly bursting into song;

and Heimdall with his golden teeth are undercharacterised, but Frigg comes into her own in *Runelight*. Readers must immerse themselves in Harris's imaginative world as if in a video game if they are to understand its complicated theology and multiple runic alphabets, but Harris's study of Old Norse pays off; there is pleasure to be had in recognising the play she makes with her mythic sources.

Maddie is too young to fall prey to sexual desire, though *Runelight*, set three years later, pitches her twin sister into turmoil when she falls in love with the wrong person. Melvin Burgess, who recalls reading Picard's versions of the heroic legend of Sigmund and Signy as a boy, faces teenage sexuality head-on in the 'thrillingly demented' *Bloodtide* (1999).[40] Excited by the power of the legends he had read – 'you always feel that the abyss is opening up at your feet' – Burgess wrote on his website that he 'didn't want to write about blokes with beards in iron helmets – I wanted to write about modern people.'[41] Burgess sets his story in a futuristic London, where the twins Siggy and Signy are the children of the warlord Val Volson, whose territory is the City of London. *Bloodtide* evolves into a political novel, for genetic experiment has produced a race of half-man, half-animal. Large questions about race, humanity and identity are opened up, as Siggy is saved by a halfwoman from the monstrous Pig (rather than the original she-wolf), which devours his brothers. Signy herself is crippled; her husband has her hamstrung, in a borrowing from the eddic poem *Völundarkviða*, yet he continues to assert how much he loves her even as he imprisons her. With the help of Cherry, a shapeshifting cat who is daughter of Loki, Signy succeeds in her vengeance against her husband, sleeping with her brother and giving birth to a child whom she has cloned and trained as a ruthless killer. Odin is a powerful presence in the novel, appearing quietly at key moments of the plot. Loki too, who does not figure in the Norse source, is also prominent; Burgess found Picard's Loki, 'crafty red-haired Loki, quick to laugh and quick to change his shape, the god of the fire that burns on the hearth', particularly compelling.[42]

In 2005 Burgess followed *Bloodtide* with *Bloodsong*, the story of Sigurd and his betrayal by his brother-in-law.[43] If *Bloodtide* is political, *Bloodsong* is theological; Sigurd undergoes a rite of passage as he lies in wait for the dragon, he dies and is reborn, and he exhibits an adolescent's sense of invincibility and idealism. Cloning once again is central to the plot, raising questions about whether Sigurd's soul is stolen, and where identity really resides. The novel ends with an astonishing *Liebestod*, but it is nevertheless starkly satisfying. Though Burgess's other novels have often courted controversy with their frank depiction of teenage sexuality and drug-taking, the violence of the two *Blood* books is, as their author observes, close enough to the aesthetic of computer games to escape moral censure.

In recent years, then, Norse myth and legend have shaken off their unhappy associations with Nazism; a generation of authors who were born in the 1950s and 1960s are engaging with the Æsir and the Volsungs on their own terms, recognising the power

of the ancient stories to enthral and to move. New writers for children have moved away from the gloomy and violent view of Norse myth which C.S. Lewis recognised in Tolkien as 'hammer-strokes but with compassion', towards an altogether more engaged, vigorous and optimistic participation in, even reshaping of, the old patterns.[44] New kinds of dystopia are imagined: Burgess's techno-nightmare, in which England just survives nuclear strikes on London; Harris's world of medieval and rural superstition, presided over by the ruins of an academic elite which has forsaken the search for knowledge for religious extremism. In some other stories, the gods are called into the present world, or something very much like it, by a surviving Norse artefact. In Francesca Simon's *The Sleeping Army* (2011) young Freya, mooching around

in the British Museum where her father is a security guard, finds herself strangely drawn to a horn lying next to the Lewis Chessmen, and blows it.[45] She is precipitated into the world of the gods and has to assist Thor's two human helpers, Thjalfi (here called Alfie) and Roskva, and a smelly berserker warrior called Snot (wise one) to rescue Idunn and her apples of immortality from the giants. Freya learns much about her capacities and does a fair bit of growing up in her race not only to save the gods, but to prevent herself and her companions from turning into chessmen themselves and joining other failed questers in the museum case (*figure 33*).

Hollywood too has used Norse artefacts: in the 1994 film *The Mask*, starring Jim Carrey, a mask belonging to Loki transforms a mild-mannered bank clerk into a manic superhero. The recent *Thor* (2011) sees Thor (Chris Hemsworth), exiled from Asgard for disobedience to Odin (Anthony Hopkins), arrive in the USA, again in search of his lost hammer.[46] The plot hinges on Thor overcoming his previous arrogance and becoming worthy to wield Mjöllnir once more. His moral growth allows him to baffle Loki's plot to turn Asgard over to the frost giants and to save Odin and the other gods.

The gods have been redefined for the twenty-first century. Loki is an anti-hero with a crooked smile; his ambivalence and queasy loyalties in his relations with gods and giants make him both complex and attractive. Odin has become kindlier and less devious; Thor, perhaps, is less bumbling, though no less mighty, assimilated as he is to the American superhero model. The Norse gods are not as familiar characters as their Greek counterparts, but their imaginative power is on the rise again. Not even Ragnarök can destroy them, as Harris shows, for as the words of the eddic poem *Völuspá* (The Seeress's Prophecy) foretell their return:

> coming up a second time,
> Earth from the ocean, eternally green …
> the Æsir meet on Idavoll … they remember there the great events …
> afterwards will be found in the grass
> the wonderful golden chequers,
> those which they possessed in ancient times.[47]

3

The magical Middle Ages
in children's fantasy literature

DAVID CLARK

A FAUN carrying an umbrella; a hobbit who lives in a hole; a mysterious name – Lyra; an ill-treated schoolboy with a scar and a secret. Children's fantasies may be said in some sense to begin with resonant images – certainly they often do so in the authors' myths of origins. However, they also begin in an author's reading practices, in his or her experiences, in the influences which, acknowledged or not, shape and articulate their own vision and help define what it is and, sometimes more importantly, what it is not.

Medieval culture and literature in one way or another have provided inspiration for all of the writers discussed in this chapter, from Anglo-Saxon warrior heroes and valiant last stands to druids and the Celtic Otherworld, from chivalric knights and more or less distressed damsels to manuscripts and scribes and the Bodleian Library itself. It is almost impossible now to think of fantasy literature without simultaneously thinking of J.R.R. Tolkien, and indeed some of the fantasy literature that followed the publication of *The Lord of the Rings* is derivative of his created world, rather than taking influence from the medieval sources upon which he drew. However, this chapter shows that medievalist fantasy existed both before and after Tolkien, and that the Middle Ages still provide a rich source for the creative imagination.

We may divide medievalist fantasy into a couple of types. First, we have fantasies of an imagined past, which divide in turn into those which seek to re-create the historical Middle Ages but add fantastic ingredients such as dragons and spells, and those which re-create the fantasy worlds of medieval authors themselves. Second, we may identify fantasies of an imagined present, where medieval characters and the medieval world invade the contemporary environment of the books' original audience, or where medieval culture shapes the creation of an alternative world. One of the fascinating things about many of the authors discussed below, however, is the extent to which they challenge and ignore generic boundaries, to create something new from something old.

George MacDonald

We start our 150-year journey with the work of George MacDonald (1824–1905), a Scottish minister who wrote an almost incredible number of books, including works of theology, sermons and realistic novels, but who is now best known for a small number of fairy tales and fantasies. Although he did not draw on the

Middle Ages explicitly to the same extent as the other authors we will consider, he can be regarded as the progenitor of twentieth-century fantasy, since, along with the medievalist William Morris's fantasy romance *The Well at the World's End* (1896), his works exerted a profound influence on J.R.R. Tolkien and C.S. Lewis, as well as the less-well-known children's author Madeleine L'Engle (1918–2007). Indeed, in his autobiography *Surprised by Joy* (1955), Lewis credited MacDonald's novel *Phantastes* (1858) with having 'baptised' his imagination, contributing to his reluctant conversion to Christianity, and famously wrote: 'I have never concealed the fact that I regarded him as my master; indeed I fancy I have never written a book in which I did not quote from him.'[1]

Perhaps the most enduringly popular of MacDonald's works today are his children's novels *The Princess and the Goblin* (1871) and *The Princess and Curdie* (1882) (*figure* 35). In these books, MacDonald creates a fairy-tale world based loosely on medieval romance and folklore where princesses and miners' sons can interact, and where goblins and magical grandmothers nestle alongside bad-tempered housekeepers and greedy servants. In the course of the novels, both the princess and Curdie learn the importance of obedience and goodness, and Curdie also learns that a person's behaviour affects the state of his or her soul, when he is given the ability to see a person's true nature when holding their hand or foot. The treacherous doctor who is poisoning the king, for instance, is a repulsive 'creeping thing', and the Lord Chamberlain's hand is 'the claw of a bird of prey'.[2] However, the paw of the ugly and terrifying

34 George MacDonald, portrait from an advertisement for *The Sunday Magazine*, October 1871.

dog Lina, who befriends and protects Curdie, is really a 'white and smooth' child's hand, and we discover that the other monstrous animals who aid him in cleansing the castle of its evil inhabitants were once men 'whom nature had treated homeopathically', but who are now presumably on the road to recovery because of their improved behaviour.[3] This idea is a literalisation of the medieval notion, explored in romances such as the thirteenth-century *King Horn*, that a man's nature is revealed by clear physical and moral signs. However, it seems to be modified by MacDonald's idea of universal salvation, where none is ultimately allowed to perish.

It is in MacDonald's adult novel *Phantastes* (1858), however, that he draws on the Middle Ages most explicitly, and where the land of Faerie is indebted to the Celtic Otherworld, and the characters of Sir Percival and the Marble Lady stem from the courtly tropes of medieval romance. MacDonald's ministerial training comes through in the many moralistic passages in his fiction, but the imaginative power of his creation is such that the moralising rarely becomes oppressive, and traces of his influence in motif, style and morality can be seen throughout the work of Lewis and Tolkien, who both took fantasy to new heights.

MacDonald was not working in a vacuum, however; several other early classics of children's

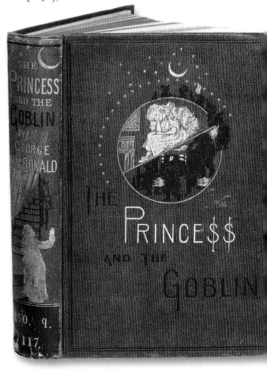

literature with fantasy elements were written in the mid-nineteenth century, from John Ruskin's Victorian fairy tale *The King of the Golden River* (1851) and Charles Kingsley's moralistic *The Water Babies* (1862) to Edward Lear's set of limericks, collected in *A Book of Nonsense* (1846), and Charles Dodgson/Lewis Carroll's *Alice's Adventures in Wonderland* (1865), which MacDonald himself encouraged Dodgson to publish.

E. Nesbit

Another major early influence on fantasy for children and children's literature in general is Edith Nesbit (1858–1924). A prolific author, publishing under the name E. Nesbit, she is best known for her series of books about the Bastable children, beginning with *The Story of the Treasure Seekers* (1899), the Psammead series, beginning with *Five Children and It* (1902), and perhaps most famously her stand-alone novel *The Railway Children* (1906). Like MacDonald, Nesbit does not draw on the Middle Ages consistently, but, as well as producing ironic manipulations of fairy-tale tropes (as, for instance, in her short story *Melisande* of 1900), she incorporates medieval scenes into her fantasy novels. In *Five Children and It*, one of the wishes the Psammead (or sand fairy) grants is for the children to have a castle. As with their other wishes, this one goes wrong and the children discover that there are distinct disadvantages to being in possession of a late medieval castle which is being besieged by the forces of Sir Wulfric de Talbot and in

35 George MacDonald, *The Princess and the Goblin*, 1872 Strahan edn, illustrated by Arthur Hughes (1832–1915). Although George MacDonald wrote hundreds of books on various topics, he is now best remembered for his children's fantasies. MacDonald had a huge influence on C.S. Lewis and J.R.R. Tolkien.

Oxford, Bodleian Library, 250 q.117, illustrated boards.

which it is extremely difficult to get any dinner. Nesbit plays the episode for laughs and neatly satirises Victorian medievalism. Sir Wulfric, for instance, is 'exactly like the pictures Robert had so often admired in the historical romances'.[4] However, Nesbit goes on: 'His armour and his weapons were all, I am almost sure, of quite different periods. The shield was thirteenth-century, while the sword was of the pattern used in the Peninsular War. The cuirass was of the time of Charles I, and the helmet dated from the Second Crusade.'[5] The only way Robert can communicate with Sir Wulfric is to recall sentences 'straight out of *Ralph de Courcy; or, The Boy Crusader*', involving such constructions as 'Gramercy for thy courtesy, fair sir knight'.[6] Nesbit is satirising the hugely popular historical adventure stories of G.A. Henty, who indulges in similar historical anachronisms and overwrought dialogue in most of his 122 novels like *The Dragon and the Raven: The Days of King Alfred* (1886), *The Boy Knight: A Tale of the Crusades* (1891), *Wulf the Saxon: A Story of the Norman Conquest* (1895) and *A March on London: Being a Story of Wat Tyler's Insurrection* (1898), which last mentions Ralph de Courcy himself. As well as satirising medievalism, however, Nesbit also produced fantasy versions of medieval bestiaries in collections such as *The Book of Beasts* (1899) and *The Book of Dragons* (1900) (*see figure* 14). She was a lasting influence on children's authors. Lewis even tells us at the start of *The Magician's Nephew* (1955) that it is set at the time that 'the Bastables were looking for treasure in the Lewisham Road'.[7] He also lifts a number of plot devices from Nesbit in this novel such as the eruption of the Babylonian Queen into contemporary London in *The Story of the Amulet* (1906) and the use of magic rings in *The Enchanted Castle* (1907). The entrance to Narnia is also prefigured by Nesbit's use of access to a magical world through a wardrobe in 'The Aunt and Amabel', a short story in her collection *The Magic World* (1912).

Rudyard Kipling

Although Rudyard Kipling (1865–1936) is better known for his *Just So Stories* (1902) and *The Jungle Book* (1894), which inspired the beloved Disney film, he also wrote *Puck of Pook's Hill* (1906) and its sequel *Rewards and Fairies* (1910), in which two children, Dan and Una, manage to conjure up Puck himself, 'the oldest Old Thing in England', and, through his offices, encounter a series of figures and crucial events from England's past. Notable among these is the story of Weland the Smith (*figure* 36), known from the Anglo-Saxon poem *Deor*; the Old Norse poem *Völundarkviða*; and a couple of references in King Alfred's Old English translation of Boethius's *Consolation of Philosophy* (regarded as one of the seminal texts of the Middle Ages). In Kipling's version, Weland was once the smith of the Norse gods, but when the English stopped worshipping the old gods and they began to disappear he degenerated into 'a white-bearded, bent old blacksmith in a leather apron', known as Wayland-Smith, waiting to be released to Valhalla by 'some human being [who] truly wishes me well'.[8] Puck tells the children how Hugh, an Anglo-Saxon novice, eventually does so and is rewarded by a magical sword that brings him good fortune. This sword later comes into the possession of Sir Richard Dalyngridge, who 'came over with William the Conqueror', and who tells the children how he and Hugh the Saxon came to be friends, and to rule together over the people who were soon to become 'neither Norman nor Saxon, but all English'.[9] Sir Richard is delighted when Dan reads to him the story of Othere's voyages (well known to medievalists in King Alfred's translation), since he recognises it 'even as I have heard the men in the Dane ships sing it'.[10] He tells the children how he and Hugh voyaged with the Danes to Africa and returned with a shipload of gold to the Castle at Pevensey. After many other encounters, the children eventually hear from Kadmiel, a Jewish moneylender, how King John signed the Magna Carta, 'the New Law at Runnymede' which will govern both Jew and Christian wisely, not because of the threats of his

36 Front panel of the eighth-century Franks Casket. The left-hand side depicts part of the story of Weland the Smith. Known variously as Weland, Wayland and Völundr, the lamed smith features in Anglo-Saxon, Old Norse, and later medieval legend, as well as Rudyard Kipling's *Puck of Pook's Hill* (1906).

© The Trustees of the British Museum.

barons, but because of his greed for money.[11] Kadmiel reveals that he had cast all of the Pevensey gold into the sea so that King John would be forced to sign the New Laws, and the common people would be saved from his oppression and cruelty. Puck tells the children: 'Weland gave the Sword! The Sword gave the Treasure, and the Treasure gave the Law. It's as natural as an oak growing.'[12] Dan and Una do not understand, but the reader sees that, for Kipling, England's history is all one story that is still unfolding today like an ancient stalwart oak, the quintessential English tree. Kipling's decision to have characters from the past invade the present is one that becomes very popular from the 1960s onwards, but until then it is more common for medievalist authors to create Secondary Worlds: imagined environments which draw on the Middle Ages as a source of inspiration, as in the work of Lewis and Tolkien.

C.S. Lewis

Where the previous authors' medievalism is found in their fiction, C.S. Lewis (1898–1963) drew on the Middle Ages in most of his writings. From the use of Dante in *The Screwtape Letters* (1942), myriad allusions in his poetry, and the re-imagination of the medieval cosmos in his Cosmic Trilogy (*Out of the Silent Planet*, 1938; *Perelandra*, 1943; and *That Hideous Strength*, 1948), Lewis rarely wrote without betraying his status as one of the twentieth century's most influential medievalists. He taught medieval and Renaissance literature at Magdalen College, Oxford, and Magdalene College, Cambridge, and his professional publications such as *The Allegory of Love: A Study in Medieval Tradition* (1936) and *The Discarded Image: An Introduction to Medieval and Renaissance Literature* (1964) are still widely read and respected. However, he is best known today for the seven children's books entitled collectively *The Chronicles of Narnia*.

Tolkien was not a fan of these books, complaining about the way that they mix elements from many different mythologies together with characters like Father Christmas, and many critics have emulated his disapproval. Recently, however, Michael Ward has argued that a secret design lies behind the series: each book relates to the attributes of one of the seven medieval planets (i.e. 'wandering' celestial bodies):

> In *The Lion* [the children] become monarchs under sovereign Jove; in *The 'Dawn Treader'* they drink light under searching Sol [the sun]; in *Prince Caspian* they harden under strong Mars; in *The Silver Chair* they learn obedience under subordinate Luna [the moon]; in *The Horse and His Boy* they come to love poetry under eloquent Mercury; in *The Magician's Nephew* they gain life-giving fruit under fertile Venus; and in *The Last Battle* they suffer and die under chilling Saturn.[13]

Although not all critics agree with Ward's thesis, it is certainly true, as Kathryn Kerby-Fulton has put it, that Lewis's lifetime endeavour was to reconstruct 'the medieval *Weltanschauung* [world-view]'; rereading the Narnia Chronicles after *The Discarded Image* brings out a new depth to Lewis's created Secondary World.[14]

Schema prædictæ diuifionis.

37 Peter Apian, *Cosmographia*, 1540. This illustration from a sixteenth-century printed book shows the 'discarded image' of the cosmos, of which C.S. Lewis wrote in his scholarship and which influenced *The Chronicles of Narnia*.

Image courtesy History of Science Collections, University of Oklahoma Libraries.

Several manuscript illustrations still survive of the medieval cosmos – the 'discarded image' of which Lewis wrote (*figure 37*). Lewis claimed that 'the old Model delights me', and his work as a whole is permeated by the influence of the medieval poet Dante.[15]

However, there are other specific medieval influences in the books: the medieval pageantry of *The Lion, the Witch and the Wardrobe*; the ringing of the bell in Charn in *The Magician's Nephew* (which recalls a similar scene in the twelfth-century French romance *Yvain*, by Chrétien de Troyes); the use in *The Voyage of the 'Dawn Treader'* of the Celtic tradition of the *immram*, or sea voyage, to the Otherworld, Reepicheep's absurd chivalry, and the fantastic creatures such as the Dufflepuds (*figure 38*), with their

38 Drawings of the Dufflepuds for a manuscript of *The Voyage of the 'Dawn Treader'* (1952). Here we see a visualization of the comic Dufflepuds from Lewis's imaginative novel, which borrows and reworks a number of legendary beings from medieval texts such as the *Marvels of the East* and *The Travels of Sir John Mandeville*.

Oxford, Bodleian Library, MS. Eng. lett. c. 220/1, fol. 161r, pen and ink. Extracts/images © C.S. Lewis Pte Ltd.

Cote Armure

Sir Gawayn

18

BRACE →
Cowters →
Sayn —
ON. Djarf fortis
> severus
Brynd
Quissewes
Polaynes →
greves →
Sabatounz
Merely graphic?

F. Aduber, ornare

Provencal.

fastened
of ME. knag, peg

Umbewese fan
(umefan, clothe)

And mony oþer menskful, with Mador de la Port.   555
Alle þis compayny of court com þe kyng nerre
For to counseyl þe knyȝt, with care at her hert.
Þere watȝ much derue doel driuen in þe sale,
Þat so worthé as Wawan schulde wende on þat ernde,
To dryȝe a delful dynt, and dele no more   560
      wyth bronde.
      Þe knyȝt mad ay god chere,
      And sayde, 'Quat schuld I wonde?   wandian, shrink
      Of destinés derf and dere
      What may mon do bot fonde?'   565

He dowelleȝ þer al þat day, and dresseȝ on þe morn,
Askeȝ erly hys armeȝ, and alle were þay broȝt.
Fyrst a tulé tapit tyȝt ouer þe flet,
And miche watȝ þe gyld gere þat glent þeralofte;
Þe stif mon steppeȝ þeron, and þe stel hondeleȝ,   570
Dubbed in a dublet of a dere tars,
And syþen a crafty capados, closed aloft,   186
Þat wyth a bryȝt blaunner was bounden withinne.   155.
Þenne set þay þe sabatounȝ vpon þe segge foteȝ,
His legeȝ lapped in stel with luflych greueȝ,   575
With polayneȝ piched þerto, policed ful clene,
Aboute his kneȝ knaged wyth knoteȝ of golde;
Queme quyssewes þen, þat coyntlych closed
His thik þrawen þyȝeȝ, with þwonges to tachched;
And syþen þe brawden bryné of bryȝt stel ryngeȝ   580
Vmbeweued þat wyȝ vpon wlonk stuffe,
And wel bornyst brace vpon his boþe armes,   Collactive Pl.
With gode cowters and gay, and gloueȝ of plate,
And alle þe godlych gere þat hym gayn schulde
            þat tyde;   585
      Wyth ryche cote-armure,
      His gold sporeȝ spend with pryde,   ON. Spenna, fasten
      Gurde wyth a bront ful sure
      With silk sayn vmbe his syde.

① ON. Mennska, humanitas > curialitas > favor > m'ful, honourable. ② The eptive forms in such contexts naturally has little eptive sense. "Drew near" ③ "Raised" mode. ④ To try > try by experience > go through with. ⑤ Intrans. "gets ready" ⑥ Red silk of Toulouse > any red stuff. ⑦ Here "drawn, spread". Trahere happens to be the first meaning in Bst Toll for OE tyhtan but Edd. think its ME. usages in general are influenced by dihtan. ⑧ OF. Tarse Turkestan ⑨ Tunic of Cappadocian leather. ⑩ þrawan > þrawen tortus > well knit ⑪ gegna prodesse. ⑫ cf Saynt (= ceint) 2431

39 C.S. Lewis's copy of J.R.R. Tolkien and E.V. Gordon's edition of *Sir Gawain and the Green Knight* (1925). This fourteenth-century text was a strong influence on both Lewis and Tolkien, who edited the poem.

Oxford, Bodleian Library, Arch. H e.55, pp. 18–19. © The J.R.R. Tolkien Estate Limited 2013.

one huge foot, who are influenced by Herodotus, *The Travels of Sir John Mandeville*, and the Anglo-Saxon *Marvels of the East*, a set of travellers' tales bound up in the same manuscript as *Beowulf*.[16] *The Silver Chair* (1953) is particularly interesting in this context, since it shows the influence of the medieval romance *Sir Gawain and the Green Knight*, edited and translated by Tolkien (*figure* 39).

Sir Gawain and the Green Knight, composed in the north-west Midlands in the fourteenth century, recounts how, in the early days of King Arthur's court, Camelot is shocked by the appearance of a huge mounted knight who is entirely green and proposes a bizarre game in which someone from the court must behead him. In return he must allow the Green Knight to behead him at a future date. Gawain, the flower of Arthurian chivalry, takes up this challenge and a year after the Green Knight's beheading and unexpected survival, he must travel to receive his own blow. On the way he stops at the castle of Hautdesert where he rests from his traumatic journey for three days, on each of which his host, Lord Bertilak, rides out to hunt, and his hostess attempts unsuccessfully to seduce him. Gawain accepts a magic green girdle from her, which she claims will preserve his life, but when he goes to meet the Green Knight it is revealed that the Green Knight is actually Bertilak in disguise, who had sent his own wife to test Gawain's strength of character. Gawain returns to Camelot a sadder but wiser man (*figure* 40).

The chivalric behaviour and speech of Prince Rilian, the son of King Caspian who has been imprisoned and enchanted below the earth of Narnia, recalls the extreme courtesy of Sir Gawain in

40 An illustration from the unique manuscript of *Sir Gawain and the Green Knight* from the mid-fourteenth century. The poem describes how a mysterious Green Knight on a green horse bursts into King Arthur's court at Camelot with an outrageous challenge: to cut off his head with his own axe and then find him a year and a day later to meet the same fate.

London, British Library, Cotton MS. Nero A. X, fol. 129v. © British Library Board.

the medieval poem. Moreover, his captor, the Lady of the Green Kirtle, is reminiscent of Gawain's temptress, the Lady of Hautdesert. We are never told the Lady's name by the *Gawain*-poet, but she is close to the enchantress Morgan le Fay, and wife to a disguised knight, and she might as well have been called the Lady of the Green Girdle. As well as using this romance, Lewis also makes a very medievalist joke when he gives one of his chapters the title 'A parliament of owls', alluding to Chaucer's poem *The Parliament of Fowls* (*c.*1382).

J.R.R. Tolkien

Sir Gawain and the Green Knight is also one of the many medieval texts on which J.R.R. Tolkien (1892–1973) drew in his fiction, as well as his professional life. It is parodied in his novella *Farmer Giles of Ham* (1969), and Miriam Youngerman Miller identifies a large number of correspondences with *The Lord of the Rings* itself. As she says:

> both works depict two-tiered Other Worlds; that is, both initial settings (Camelot and the Shire) are secondary to the reader, but are nonetheless primary to the chief characters (Gawain and the hobbits) who are then taken on their journeys into further worlds which are secondary to them and tertiary to us. In both cases, both the audience and the characters experience that sense of wonder which Tolkien calls Faërie.[17]

Lewis and Tolkien share a technique for creating a sense of realism in their fantasy by the use of richly described detail (as in

41 As well as writing novels, Tolkien lectured in Anglo-Saxon at Oxford; after his death his edition of this poetic version of the Biblical book of Exodus was published (1981). The word *middangeard*, found at the beginning of the poem, means 'Middle-earth', and Old English is the language of the Rohirrim, or Riders of Rohan.

Oxford, Bodleian Library, MS. Tolkien A 22/1, fol. 121. © The J.R.R. Tolkien Estate Limited 2013.

Exodus.

HWÆT WE FEOR J NEAH gefrigen habbað
ofer middangeard Moyses dómas
wrætlico wordriht wera cneorissum ——
in uprodor eadigra gehwam
5 æfter bealusiðe bote lifes,
lifigendra gehwam langsumne ræd —
hæleðum secgan : gehýre se ðe wille!

Þone on westenne Weroda Drihten,
sóðfæst Cyning, mid his sylfes miht
10 gewyrðode, and him wundra fela
éce Alwalda in æht forgeaf.
He wæs leof Gode leoda aldor,
horse and hreðergleaw herges wísa,
freom foletoga. Faraónes cyn,
15 Godes andsacan, gyrdwite band,
þær him gesealde sigora Waldend
modgum magoræswan his mága feorh,
onwist eðles Abrahames sunum.

Poem begins on p.143 of MS. First line has the 'canto-number' xlii', above
neah. 23 and and a half lines follow, vv. 1-29 (wiston). Then a line and
a half an blank.   1, Hwæt — neah in capitals, with large ornamental
initial H. habbað : habad.   3, wrætlico : wrælico ⁊ hæleðu 8,
~~andsaca~~ werode. 15 andsaca.   17 magoræswum. 18 onwist.

the introduction of the Green Knight), and just as the Castle of Hautdesert appears in response to need, so does Tom Bombadil's cottage, and Bertilak and Tom are similar in appearance and of a similarly ambiguous morality. Snow blizzards are the most formidable obstacles for both Gawain and Frodo in their journeys, and both heroes receive tempting offers at the side of waterfalls to relinquish their quests, Gawain from the Guide, and Frodo from Boromir. Both heroes discover that, in the end, it is their character that has been tested and both are left with physical and mental scars from their ordeals, discovering when they return home that they no longer fit in. The major difference here, of course, is that it is not the courtly hero but the seemingly insignificant hobbit who is the central protagonist, and this fits in with Tolkien's wider tendency to celebrate the 'little' man. *Sir Gawain and the Green Knight* is, of course, far from being the only medieval influence on Tolkien's work. Tolkien critics have written ever more thorough studies of the historical models for Tolkien's invented languages (such as the Elvish languages' debts to Welsh and Finnish) and place names and character names (such as Eärendil, based on a learned etymological and mythological reading of a name in the Anglo-Saxon poem *Christ*, by Cynewulf). They have also identified his influences and reworkings of medieval texts on the level of theme, character and plot. As Jane Chance and David Day summarise, what has become increasingly clear about Tolkien is

the breadth of his learning – his knowledge of Old and Middle High German, Icelandic, Dutch, Swedish, Finnish, and Old Norse,

42 This is Tolkien's own drawing of the Hall of Beorn, for *The Hobbit* (1937). Beorn is the shape-shifting bear of a man whose name comes from the Old English for 'man', 'hero', or 'warrior', just one of the many instances of Tolkien's medieval influences.

Oxford, Bodleian Library, MS. Tolkien Drawings 15. © The J.R.R. Tolkien Estate Limited 2013.

Fire
light
in
Beorn's
hou
se

Welsh, Celtic, and Old English, and Latin – and of his reading – his use of the Eddas, the *Kalevala*, *Beowulf*, *The Battle of Maldon*, *The Ancrene Riwle*, Chaucerian *fabliaux*, *Sir Gawain and the Green Knight*, the Percival story in its various medieval redactions, the *Confessio Amantis*, the *Morte D'Arthur*, and the Latin works of medieval Christian thinkers.[18]

What is fascinating, too, is to see how Tolkien critics are often also medievalists, teaching and studying the same material that Tolkien did, and sometimes also writers of medievalist children's fantasy, as with Verlyn Flieger, whose first novel, *Pig Tale* (2002), reworks Celtic myth and legend, and who has written on Tolkien and medieval literature for many years.

The 'Oxford' School

Following Lewis and Tolkien, other writers who studied at the University of Oxford also tapped into the rich vein afforded by the Middle Ages, particularly Susan Cooper in her *The Dark Is Rising* sequence (1965–77) and Alan Garner in his children's fantasies. Both are eclectic in their incorporation of Anglo-Saxon, later medieval, Norse and Celtic elements in their work: particularly in Garner's *The Weirdstone of Brisingamen* (1960).

One under-examined influence in Cooper's *The Dark Is Rising* (1973), seldom noticed by critics and elided (along with much else) in the disappointing 2007 film *The Seeker* (dir. David L. Cunningham), is that of the artefact known as the Alfred Jewel, housed in the Ashmolean Museum in Oxford (*figure* 43). It is often identified with the *æstels* which King Alfred sent to accompany translations of Pope Gregory the Great's *Pastoral Care*, one of the books he considered 'most needful for men to know' and which he thought would help in the intellectual and cultural revival of England, devastated by Viking raids and by what he considered to be moral and intellectual laziness. In *The Dark Is Rising*, the fifth of the Six Signs, the Sign of Fire, has the parallel inscription *Liht mec heht gewyrcan*, which Merriman Lyon [Merlin] translates as 'The Light ordered that I should be made.'[19] As Michael Drout argues, both King Alfred and King Arthur, as Lords of the Light, represent for Cooper national heroes who held off invasions of the island of Britain by the forces of darkness, violence and ignorance, and she also reworks elements of Old English poetry (in *The Dark Is Rising* and *Greenwitch*), especially from *Beowulf* (in the ship burial associated with the Sign of Water).[20]

The Vikings appear throughout the sequence as marauding invaders, the Anglo-Saxons as beleaguered craftsmen, but the Celts and Wales are the richest source of her fantasy, in terms of time (pagan festival days are crucial to each of the novels), place (Logres and Wales are key settings) and plot. Celtic characters such as Taliesin, Arthur, Owain Glyndŵr, and the *afanc* and *Mari Llwyd* permeate *Silver on the Tree*, which adapts the 'Tale of Taliesin'. Like Kipling, Cooper has a sense that Britain is innately connected to its past. She has spoken of her love of Wales in particular:

43 The Alfred Jewel. This beautiful ninth-century object in gold, quartz and enamel, is inscribed with the words *Ælfred mec het gewyrcan* (Alfred commanded me to be made). A similar inscribed magical object is found in Susan Cooper's *The Dark Is Rising* (1973).

You walk those mountains and the sense of the past is all around you. And I intend to write from that kind of awareness. The magic, if you like, is all around.[21]

This sense of place connecting past and present is also crucial to Alan Garner's work, with its intrinsic use of his native Cheshire. He, too, however, was captivated by Celtic myth and in *The Owl Service* (1967) he expands the last episode of the Fourth Branch of the *Mabinogion* so that the modern love triangle of Gwyn, Alison and Roger repeats the disastrous dynamic of Lleu, his flower bride Blodeuwedd, and Gronw Bebyr. This novel is unusual in being inspired by an object – a dinner service where the decorations on the plates can be read either as flowers or as owls (*figure 44*). As well as immersing himself in Celtic mythology, Garner also did much ornithological research on owls, and this detailed work is characteristic of his method in writing all of his books. Indeed, only a fraction of his research makes its way into the finished novels, and what is there is not obtrusive, as we can see from a rare copy of the annotated text of *Elidor* (1965) presented to Naomi Lewis and now in the Bodleian (Alan Garner Collection (BYU) Box 6, Item 7), in which Garner points out both conscious and unconscious literary allusions.

Like George MacDonald, Garner is heavily influenced by folk tale and legend (*figure 45*). *Elidor* is based on an amalgamation of several sources, from the Welsh folk tale 'Elidor and the Golden Ball', described in Giraldus Cambrensis's *Itinerarium Cambriae* (1188), and the English folk tales 'Childe Rowland' and 'Burd

44 The plate designs pictured here were drawn by Griselda Garner from the plate which inspired Alan Garner's novel *The Owl Service* (1967): the decorations can be interpreted as flowers or as owls. His novel reworks a tragic love triangle from the medieval Welsh *Mabinogion*.

Oxford, Bodleian Library, Alan Garner Collection (Archive), Box 16, number 26. © Griselda Greaves.

Ellen', to the Four Treasures of the Tuatha Dé Danann and the Land of Tir-nan-Og from Irish mythology. The traditional myth of the unicorn that can only be tamed by a young maiden is fused here with religious symbolism, and chapter 12 alludes to the fifteenth-century lyric of the Virgin birth 'I sing of a mayde that is makeles' (I sing of a maiden that is matchless/pure). In *Elidor* we get the similar phrase 'Save mayde that is makeles, / Noe man

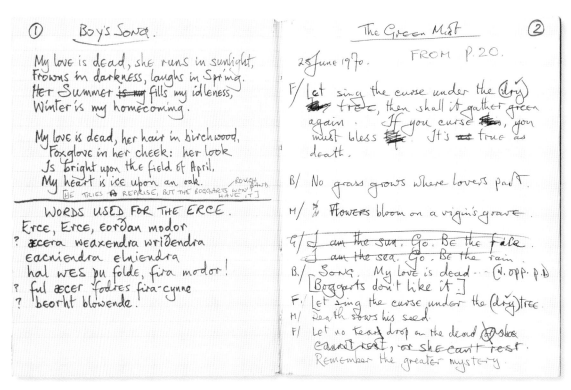

with me mell' (Except a maiden who is matchless/pure, no man may converse with me).[22] The final book of the *Weirdstone* trilogy, the recently published adult novel *Boneland*, draws strongly on *Sir Gawain and the Green Knight*, a poem composed in Garner's own region (as noted above).[23] The novel's epigraph cites the poem in a modern English version; one strand of *Boneland* takes place in and around Ludcruck, modern Ludchurch, the probable site of the Green Knight's 'chapel', and close by Alderley Edge.

Garner is not just influenced by medieval myth and traditional folk tale in his novels, however; he has also edited or reworked British (and world) folklore, for instance in *A Book of Goblins*

45 Garner's borrowings from folktale and medieval literature show an extensive knowledge and range of influence. This quotation of an Anglo-Saxon charm is found in one of the many notebooks in which Garner recorded his research and which are now in the Bodleian Library's collection.

Oxford, Bodleian Library, Alan Garner Collection (BYU), Box 5, Folder 1, Notebook 4, opened to back page. © Alan Garner.

(1969), *The Guizer: A Book of Fools* (1975) and *Alan Garner's Book of British Fairy Tales* (1984). In *Holly from the Bongs: A Nativity Play* (1966), he recast the story of Christ's birth using alliterative verse derived from the Anglo-Saxon poetic tradition and set it in the Cheshire village of Goostrey for the children of his local school (the Bongs is the name of a valley to the north of Goostrey).

Medievalist fantasy up to the present day

Celtic myth and British folklore were also major sources for Lloyd Alexander and Diana Wynne Jones (1934–2011), two of the best-known and most popular proponents of what has come to be called High Fantasy. In his *Chronicles of Prydain* (1964–68), for instance, Alexander creates a rich secondary world peopled with Celtic characters and narrative elements from *The Mabinogion*: Taran, Eilonwy, Gwydion, Gurgi, and the Crochan, or Black Cauldron, itself. The second book in the sequence, *The Black Cauldron* (1965), became a rather dissimilar Disney film in 1985. Folklore is the main source for Diana Wynne Jones's *Fire and Hemlock* (1985), which is a subtle reworking of the late medieval ballads 'Tam Lin' and 'Thomas the Rhymer', in which the heroine Polly discovers that her memories may be unreliable and that these very ballads hold the key to a true understanding of her past and the potential for a happy future. As with Garner's *The Owl Service*, here the medieval past and the contemporary present are inextricably intertwined. Jones draws on medieval culture for several other of her novels, and has the distinction of being one of the few best-selling medievalist fantasy authors to have written a critical piece on reworking the Middle Ages, as befits someone who, like Susan Cooper, attended Lewis's and Tolkien's lectures. Jones is not an uncritical medievalist, however, and her *Tough Guide to Fantasyland* (1996) satirises, in Rough Guide style, many of the medievalist clichés found among less discerning followers of Tolkien.

In *Fire and Hemlock*, Jones delineates a strong female protagonist who takes charge of her own destiny, and other authors of the 1980s and 1990s also present a revisionary take on traditional gender roles. Although Ursula Le Guin characterises her own best-selling *Wizard of Earthsea* trilogy (1968–72) as being limited by unquestioned patriarchal assumptions, she later added a fourth and then a fifth book to the series, *Tehanu* (1990) and *The Other Wind* (2001), which feature more complex and autonomous female protagonists and explore some of the ideas about gender and sexual identity she influentially questioned in her adult science-fiction novels such as *The Left Hand of Darkness* (1969), which won both the Hugo and the Nebula Award.

The *Alanna* novels of Tamora Pierce (1983–88) are set in a fantasy world clearly based on medieval Europe, but in which the heroine, Alanna, refuses the traditional female roles available in this social context, and disguises herself as a boy, Alan, in order to train as a knight. It is not just girls who resist gender stereotyping, however. Alanna's brother Thom hates fighting as much as Alanna loves it, and it is his place as a knight that Alanna takes so that he can journey to the City of the Gods to become a sorcerer. As the novels progress, Alanna learns to explore and accept her full potential as both a martial champion and a woman, becoming a complex and powerful individual who challenges the strict social hierarchy of her world, based on the structure of the high Middle Ages of kings and queens, knights and squires, servants and slaves.

A girl also disguises herself as a boy in order to avoid the limitations imposed upon her sex in Terry Jones's *The Knight and the Squire* (1997), where the main protagonist, Tom, learns the dangers of making assumptions as he and his friend Alan run off for a life of excitement and adventure at the time of the Crusades. Although Jones's novels are set in the historical Middle Ages, he includes elements of fantasy, such as wolves that can communicate with and want to help trusted humans. A similar mix of history with fantasy or magic seems to be the rule in much children's fiction of the last twenty years or so, as for example in Sherryl Jordan's *The Raging Quiet* (2000), Katy Moran's *Bloodline* (2008) and Theresa Tomlinson's *Wolf Girl* (2006). One of the most intriguing of these is Catherine Fisher's *Snow-Walker Trilogy* (1993–96), where the most pervasive influence comes from Norse mythology, including chapter headings from the Old Norse mythological poem *Hávamál*. However, the second book in the trilogy, *The Empty Hand* (1995), is based structurally on the Old English epic *Beowulf*, and most of the chapter headings are translations or reworkings of sentences or phrases from this and other Anglo-Saxon poems. Chapter 1, for instance, begins with the heading 'Darkness drowns everything and under its shadow-cover shapes… glide dark beneath the clouds'.[24] This quotation from the Old English poem *The Wanderer* has been modified slightly to be reminiscent of the lines describing Grendel's approach to the golden hall Heorot in *Beowulf*, and this fits the chapter's opening focus on a nameless creature, aching with hunger, and eager for 'the sweetness of meat, the warmth of blood'.[25] The hunt for this beast is closely modelled on the passage in *Beowulf* where the warriors follow Grendel's tracks, but Fisher's monster does not have a mother, as does Grendel in the Anglo-Saxon poem. Similarly, the novel does not focus on a hero and stereotypically masculine traits of physical bravery and demonstrations of power. Instead, it is interested in the heroism of ordinary people, including a nobly born and courageous girl, Jessa, who learns to value and respect a thrall, Hakon, and the climax is one in which Kari, in facing the rune-beast, confronts his own hunger for meaning and revenge, and manages to resist the desire to use power for selfish ends and learns the value of the empty hand.

At present, the best-known children's books with medieval elements are Philip Pullman's *His Dark Materials* trilogy (1995–2000) and J.K. Rowling's phenomenally popular *Harry Potter* series (1997–2007). Their popularity does not rest solely on their originality, however. Rowling is self-consciously reworking the tradition of the school story, with her characteristic blend of magical Otherness, puns and knowing side-swipes at the world we know (such as the substitution of OWLS for GCSEs, and the satire on government bureaucracy in the Ministry of Magic). Pullman, on the other hand, represents a sort of Milton-of-our-time with his Blakean reworking of *Paradise Lost*, but he seems to be just as influenced by his well-publicised dislike of C.S. Lewis's *Chronicles of Narnia* and what they stand for. In a sense, his is a sort of anti-medievalism, which rejects the assumptions of the Middle Ages, of Lewis the medievalist, and indeed Oxford the medieval city (*figure* 46). Lyra's world is, from one perspective, one in which the Reformation did not happen and in which the medieval Church retained its dominance and developed along the lines suggested by the Inquisition. Pullman claims to be of the devil's party, yet Charles Butler wonders if he is actually 'of C.S. Lewis's party without knowing it', and points out how, in rejecting the 'Christian–Romantic' model which favours protagonists who are too good to live, or in which children are killed off in order to avoid puberty, Pullman simultaneously preserves its structure.[26] Although the last in his trilogy does not fully succeed in tying up the strands of his previous books, and indeed validates self-sacrifice and denial as much as Lewis's novels, his worlds have imaginative breadth and depth, and will remain relevant and popular.

A similarly eclectic approach to the Middle Ages is taken by the latest generation of medievalist fantasies. A.J. Lake's *Darkest Age* series fuses Anglo-Saxon and Viking elements with dragons and magic, beginning with *The Coming of Dragons* (2006), and continuing with *The Book of the Sword* (2008) and *The Circle of Stone* (2008). As the map at the beginning of the first book indicates, this is an

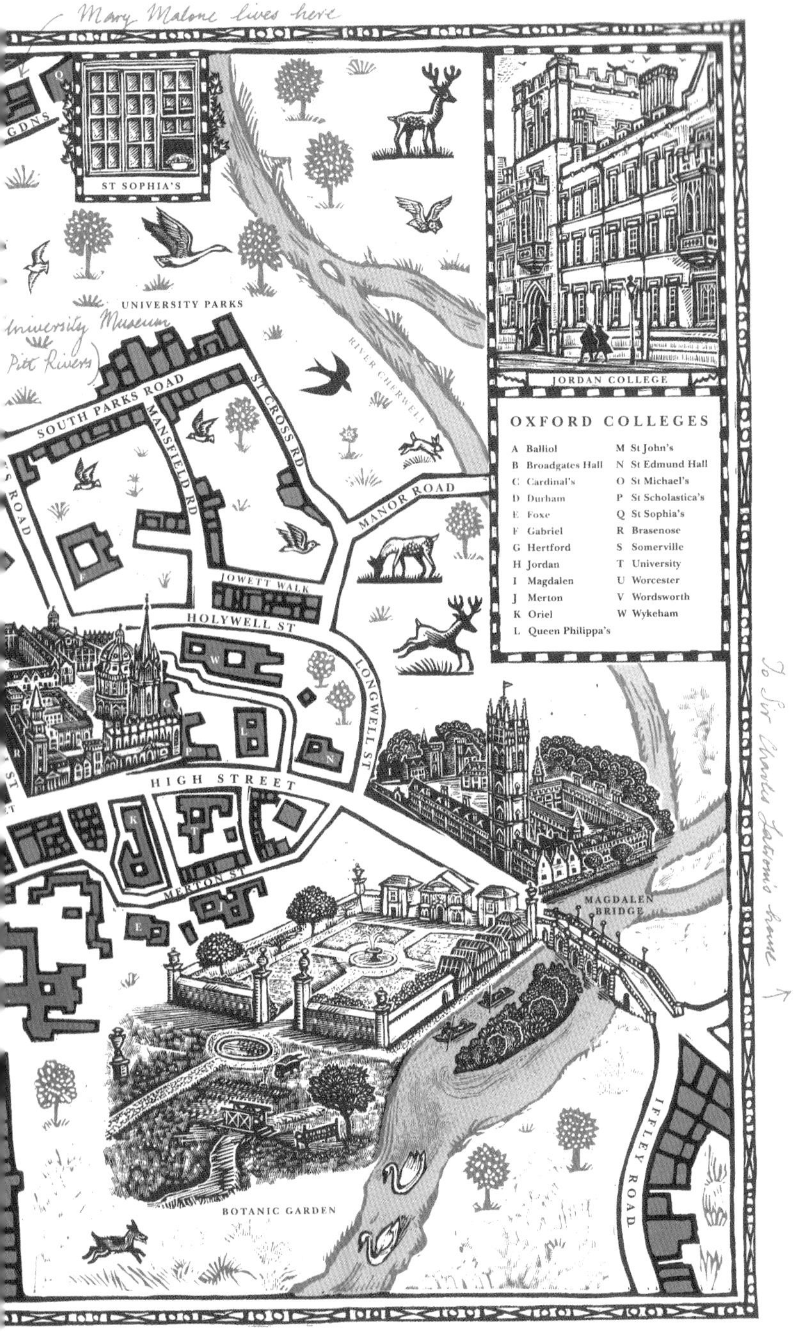

Handwritten annotations on the map:
- Mary Malone lives here
- University Museum
- Pitt Rivers
- To Sir Charles Latrom's house

Map labels:
ST SOPHIA'S

UNIVERSITY PARKS

RIVER CHERWELL

SOUTH PARKS ROAD
MANSFIELD RD
ST CROSS RD
MANOR ROAD
JOWETT WALK
HOLYWELL ST
LONGWELL ST
HIGH STREET
MERTON ST

JORDAN COLLEGE

MAGDALEN BRIDGE

BOTANIC GARDEN

IFFLEY ROAD

OXFORD COLLEGES

A	Balliol	M	St John's
B	Broadgates Hall	N	St Edmund Hall
C	Cardinal's	O	St Michael's
D	Durham	P	St Scholastica's
E	Foxe	Q	St Sophia's
F	Gabriel	R	Brasenose
G	Hertford	S	Somerville
H	Jordan	T	University
I	Magdalen	U	Worcester
J	Merton	V	Wordsworth
K	Oriel	W	Wykeham
L	Queen Philippa's		

46 Philip Pullman's Oxford represents an alternative version of the city where the Reformation never happened and in which the medieval Church retained its dominance. The manuscript for *Lyra's Oxford* is now at the Bodleian Library (MS. Eng. C. 7801).

Map illustration by John Lawrence taken from *Lyra's Oxford* by Philip Pullman, published by David Fickling Books and designed by Trickett & Webb, 2003.

imaginative reconstruction of the so-called 'Dark Age' Britain of the seventh or eighth century, where we find institutions like the 'King's Rede' and a harp-accompanied recitation of 'The Wanderer's Lament' (again, the Old English poem *The Wanderer*).[27] Similarly, Nancy Farmer's *The Sea of Trolls* (2004) features a mixed cast of Saxons, Northmen (Vikings), magical animals, trolls, and both the Norns (from Norse legend) and Grendel (from the Old English poem *Beowulf*). These books refuse to acknowledge the traditional genre boundaries of historical fiction and fantasy, and can often more suitably be termed works of magic(al) realism, where a realistic environment unproblematically embraces elements that most would consider to be supernatural or fantastic.

What is also common to all of these novels from the last twenty years is that they explore and call attention to important contemporary issues such as gender and the need to protect the environment. These fantasies also draw attention to the value of the individual, particularly those people who are outsiders because of the ways in which they are different from others – those differences often turn out to be the very thing that the world needs. As such, medievalist fantasies are empowering for children – they show that any individual is capable of heroism or cowardice, loyalty or treachery, self-sacrifice or selfishness. They also demonstrate the ways in which different people, different ways of being, different religions, and different cultures can coexist, based on a respect for others and a willingness to embrace and explore the unique potential within ourselves.

4

Once and future Arthurs: Arthurian literature for children

RITING in the first decade of the twentieth century, Lord
Robert Baden-Powell declared to his fledgling Boy Scout
troops that 'every man or boy who goes out into the world is
a knight'.[1] Seeking role models that would inspire his young
charges to the feats of physical prowess, courage, self-denial and
courtesy that he believed necessary to shore up an increasingly
unsteady Empire, Baden-Powell settled upon a hero who had
already provided inspiration for hundreds of years – King Arthur.[2]
In manuals such as *Scouting for Boys* (1908) and *Yarns for Boy Scouts*
(1909) Baden-Powell identified Arthur as 'the founder of British
Scouts'.[3] He stressed that 'the scout laws of to-day' were based
upon the rules of the Round Table.[4] As his movement grew, many
Scouting publications continued to feature adapted versions of the
Arthurian legends for use as campfire stories at Scout meetings or
gatherings. Knighthood and Arthurianism proved to be flexible
ideological tools – knightliness and imperialism are explicitly

THE
YOUNG KNIGHTS
of the
EMPIRE
BY
Sir Robert Baden-Powell

HONOUR GOD AND THE KING

OBEY THE LAW OF THE SCOUTS

DO A GOOD TURN TO SOMEBODY EVERY DAY

1/- NET

47 'You know what
a knight is ... a
gallant fellow who
was always ready to
defend weaker people.'
Published in 1916,
Robert Baden Powell's
*Young Knights of the
Empire* encouraged
the 'boy-men' of the
Scouts to identify both
themselves and the
soldiers fighting on the
front with St George,
Arthur and other
knightly figures.

Oxford, Bodleian Library,
38483 e.42, title page.

linked in *Scouting for Boys* when Baden-Powell asserts that the crusader 'King Richard I ... was one of the first Scouts of the Empire', while a patriotic image of St George dominates the cover art of the World War I-era Scouting handbook *Young Knights of the Empire* (*figure 47*).[5]

Yet Baden-Powell's use of the Arthurian story marks only one of many peaks in the popularity of Arthur over the past five centuries. Arthurian storytelling has traditionally existed on the borders of what can be considered adult and 'children's' literature, as demonstrated in works ranging from Tennyson's *Idylls* to modern-day film and comic-book adaptations. From at least the time of William Caxton (*c.* 1485), it has been concerned with role-modelling and the instilling of good behaviour in its readers, making it a useful means of providing children with instruction as well as entertainment. Yet the romantic and sexual elements of the story – Arthur's conception outside wedlock, the incestuous birth of his son (and nephew) Mordred, the adulterous love between Lancelot and Guinevere – have often proved more problematic for those writing for child audiences. The values thought to be acceptable and desirable in children's reading have changed over time, and thus the 'Arthurian legend' has evolved to mirror these changes.

Medieval Arthur

While the question of Arthur's historical existence remains problematic, it is immediately apparent that Arthurian *stories*

– whether presented as truth or as fiction – have been around for a very long time. As early as *c.*610 CE, the Brythonic history *Y Gododdin* compares the warrior Gwawrddur with the hero, deciding that he is good, but 'no Arthur'.[6] Arthur continued to appear in Latin and Welsh chronicles from the ninth to the eleventh century. In *c.*1136, Geoffrey of Monmouth completed his *Historia Regum Britanniae* (History of the Kings of Britain), introducing many elements that would be recognisable to an Arthurian reader today – including the figure of Merlin, Arthur's Roman campaign, and Arthur's final retreat to Avalon.[7] By *c.*1155 Wace's *Roman de Brut* added the Round Table and elements of 'chivalry' to the story, a process that was later completed by the English Laȝamon in *c.*1190–1215.[8] These British Arthurian stories were combined with the French traditions of Chrétien de Troyes, the *Queste del Saint Graal* and other sources to form the base material for the English-speaking Middle Ages' last – and arguably greatest – Arthuriad: Thomas Malory's massive Arthurian prose text, completed in 1469–70 and printed in 1485 by William Caxton, who gave it the title by which readers know it today – *Le Morte Darthur*.

Unlike Malory's original text, which today survives only in the 'Winchester Manuscript' rediscovered in 1934, Caxton's edition was not geared to an audience of seasoned knights. Instead, the printer appears to have explicitly repackaged the Arthurian story as a source of instruction on good behaviour and lordly/ladylike conduct for those who wished to learn the ways of their perceived social superiors. Appealing to a newly emerging London mercantile class, Caxton announces in his preface that learning about Arthur and his knights will 'brynge you to good fame and renommee' (bring you to good fame and renown), if you emulate the good deeds of the characters 'and leve the evyl' (and leave the evil). For perhaps the first time – but certainly not the last – Arthurian literature was being presented to a mass audience as a template for good conduct. Moreover, while Caxton does not explicitly address children in his Preface, there is no reason to suspect that they would not have read his *Morte* – indeed, as later commentators would point out, it is in many ways strongly appealing to child and adolescent readers.[9]

After the Middle Ages

Roger Ascham's *The Scholemaster*, published in 1570, made it clear that sixteenth-century children were indeed consuming Caxton's text – but not necessarily in the way that the printer had envisioned![10] Ascham, formerly tutor to the young Princess Elizabeth, expressed particular disapproval of that disreputable text 'Morte Arthure: the whole pleasure of which booke standeth in two speciall poyntes, in open mans slaughter, and bold bawdrye'.[11] He admits that Arthurian literature may be suitable for adult readers, as 'good stuffe, for wise men to laughe at', but stresses that it is utterly inappropriate for children: 'What toyes, the dayly readyng of such a booke, may worke in the will of a yong ientleman, or a yong mayde … wise men can iudge, and honest men do pitie.'[12]

Ascham also lists Malory's text as belonging to 'our forefathers tyme, whan Papistrie, as a standyng poole, couered and ouerflowed all England', suggesting that the coming of the Reformation in England put a temporary end to the suitability of Arthurian storytelling for child readers.[13]

While Arthurian elements are present in Spenser's *The Faerie Queene* (1590–96), they are largely downplayed. Milton considered

48 William Stansby's edition of Malory's *Morte Darthur* (1634) would be the last until the nineteenth century. It became a treasured possession of many early Arthurian enthusiasts, including Robert Southey.

King *Arthur* and his valiant Knights of the Rounnd *Table*.
Sir Triftram.   *Sir* Launcelot.   *Sir* Galahad.   *Sir* Perciuall.
Sir Gauwin.   *Sir* Ector.   *Sir* Bors.   *Sir* Lionell.   *Sir* Griffet.
Sir Gaheris.   *Sir* Tor.   *Sir* Acolon.   *Sir* Ewaine.   *Sir* Marhaus.
Sir Pelleas   *Sir* Sagris.   *Sir* Turqnine.   *Sir* Kay.   *Sir* Gareth.

Sir Beaumaus.   *Sir* Berfunt.   *Sir* Palamide.   *Sir* Belcobus.
Sir Ballamore.   *Sir* Galohalt.   *Sir* Lamarecke.   *Sir* Floll.
Sir Superablilis.   *Sir* Paginet.   *Sir* Belvoure.

THE MOST
ANCIENT AND
FAMOVS HISTORY
OF THE RENOWNED
PRINCE
ARTHVR
King of *Britaine*,

Wherein is declared his Life and Death, with all his glorious *Battailes against* the Saxons, Saracens *and* Pagans, which (for the honour of his Country) he moft worthily atchieued.

As also, all the *Noble Acts, and Heroicke* Deeds of his Valiant K N I G H T S of the R O V N D T A B L E.

Newly refined, and publifhed for the delight, and profit of the R E A D E R.

LONDON,
Printed by *William Stansby*, for *Iacob Bloome*, 1634.

49 (*overleaf top*) Some interest in Arthur survived into the seventeenth century. Here, Nathaniel Crouch holds 'Arthur the Great and Worthy British King' up as one of the 'Nine Worthies', famous men throughout history whose examples the reader should emulate. The illustrations and rhyming diction may suggest a child or adolescent readership.

Nathaniel Crouch, *The History of the Nine Worthies of the World* (1687). Oxford, Bodleian Library, Johnson f.1238, pp. 126–7.

50 (*overleaf bottom*) Arthur's court became the setting for the adventures of Tom Thumb in seventeenth-century chapbooks or 'cheap books'. These books comprise some of the earliest writing printed and sold explicitly for children. Here, Tom sets out as a Knight of the Round Table, complete with full-sized horse!

Frontispiece of *Tom Thumbe, His Life and Death*, John Wright, 1630. Oxford, Bodleian Library, 8° L 79(8) Art.

beginning a poem on 'the kings of my native land, and Arthur … or the noble-hearted heroes of the Round Table', but eventually abandoned this project.[14] An edition of Malory's text was printed by Jacob Bloome and William Stansby in 1634 – the last that would be produced until the beginning of the Arthurian revival in 1816 (*figure* 48). However, towards the end of the seventeenth century, Nathaniel Crouch's *The History of the Nine Worthies of the World* (1687) appeared (*figure* 49). Crouch stresses the importance of Arthur as an English hero, and argues that the fantastical nature of the stories should not be a reason to dismiss them: although

> The British Writers have related such strange and miraculous Actions and Adventures of this worthy Prince, that many intelligent Men have been apt to think all which hath been written of his Heroick Deeds is meer Fiction and Invention … we may be thought guilty of Incredulity and Ingratitude to deny or doubt the honourable Acts of our victorious *Arthur*.[15]

An intriguing usage of the fantasy elements of the Arthurian story also appears in some of the earliest children's picture books – the 'Tom Thumb' chapbooks, or 'cheap books', published in the late sixteenth and early seventeenth centuries. These books combined large pictures, simple stories and relatively low prices to appeal to a mass child audience. In many of the stories, the hero Tom Thumb's career includes achieving recognition as a knight at Arthur's court, either as a spur to further adventures or as the triumphant conclusion of his career (*figure* 50).

Arthur *King* of Britain.

ARthur the Great and Worthy *British* King
Glory and Victory to his Realm did bring.
He th' Heathen *Saxons* often overcame,
Inducing them to own the Christian Name.
He while he liv'd upheld the sinking State,
And Conquest seem'd upon him still to wait,
His Subjects Love thereby he doth attain,
And he must chuse one after him to Reign.
The *Pictish* King this Choice doth much resent,
As if to wrong him of his Rights they meant
Both King's ingage in Fight, where both Kings dy'd
With thousands of their Subjects on each side.

The

Tom Thumbe,

His Life and Death:

Wherein is declared many Maruailous
Acts of Manhood, full of wonder,
and strange merriments :

Which little Knight liued in King *Arthurs* time, and
famous in the Court of *Great-Brittaine*.

London Printed for *Iohn Wright.* 1630.

rthur *King of* Britain.
...ethy of the World.

...ers have related such strange
...s Actions and Adventures of
...hat many intelligent Men have
...all which hath been written
...s is meer Fiction and Inventi-
...opinion that there never was
...hough Historians disagree about
...e writing carelesly and others
...ey all all agree upon the Prede-
...t of this noble King: But as it
...delity to doubt that there was
...ism to question if there were a
...ble to deny the being of *Judas*
...be judged folly to affirm there
...ander, *Julius Cæsar*, *Godfrey* of
..., so we may be thought guilty
...gratitude to deny or doubt the
...ur victorious *Arthur*. This is
...on of our *Hero*, and his immor-
...whereby he justly gained the
...Worthy of the World. Now

...n had for above four hundred
...n subject to the *Romans*, which
...st that *Julius Cæsar* made here
...*elan* King of the *Britains* seven-
...e birth of our Blessed Saviour,
...me of the Emperor *Gratianus*,
...ty six years after Christ; *Vor-*
...Royal of the British Kings, by
...Murther of *Constance* the Son of
...pon the Crown, who growing
F 4   odious

The Arthurian revival

One of the first authors inspired by Thomas Percy's mid-eighteenth-century publication of the *Reliques of Ancient English Poetry* (1765) was Sir Walter Scott (1771–1832).[16] References to Sir Lancelot and the Holy Grail appear in the first canto of Scott's *Marmion* (1808), and his *The Bridal of Triermain* (1813) features Sir Roland de Vaux's efforts to rescue Gyneth, the illegitimate daughter of King Arthur. While Scott's historical novels and poems were intended for an adult readership, they were frequently taken up by child readers, a process that was accelerated by the production of chapbooks and dramatic adaptations of his works.[17] The poet Robert Southey (1774–1843) was also inspired both by Scott and by his childhood experiences as a reader of Malory. Southey recalled that 'when I was a schoolboy I possessed a wretchedly imperfect copy [of the 1634 edition], and there was no book, except the Faery Queen, which I perused so often, or with such deep contentment.'[18] In 1817, Southey was spurred by these memories, and by Scott's scholarly edition of the medieval poem *Sir Tristrem*, to re-edit and reprint Malory's text. He mentions in passing that, were it to be modernised 'and published as a book for boys, it could hardly fail of regaining its popularity'.[19] A similar reissue had been made the year before by the printers Walker and Edwards, confirming that a revival of Arthurian writing was at hand.

The most famous writer of the nineteenth-century Arthurian revival – and arguably the most influential on the development

THE LADY OF SHALOTT.

PART I.

I.

On either side the river lie
Long fields of barley and of rye,
That clothe the wold and meet the sky;
And thro' the field the road runs by
     To many-tower'd Camelot;

51 When creating a 'deluxe' edition of Tennyson's poems in 1857, the publisher Edward Moxon commissioned illustrations from emerging artists such as William Holman Hunt and Dante Gabriel Rossetti. Tennyson's Arthurian themes proved hugely influential on the 'Pre-Raphaelite Brotherhood' with which both artists would be involved. Here, the design first seen in Hunt's 1857 illustration for Tennyson's 'The Lady of Shalott' re-emerges in his much later painting of the same title.

Tennyson, *Poems* (1857), Oxford, Bodleian Library, Dunston B 1795, p. 67.
The Lady of Shalott, Holman Hunt, c. 1886–1905.
© Manchester City Art Galleries, 1934.401 (oil on canvas).

of Arthur literature for children – was Alfred, Lord Tennyson (1809–1892). Like Southey, Tennyson was deeply interested in Arthurian literature from boyhood.[20] In 1832–33, he produced his first set of Arthurian poems: 'The Lady of Shalott', 'Sir Launcelot and Queen Guinevere' (which now survives only in fragments) and 'Sir Galahad'. By 1855, he had begun work on the longer *Idylls of the King*, first published (later revised) in 1859, and the entirety of his Arthurian poems were collected together in the Imperial Library edition of Tennyson's *Works* (1872–73), with the exception of the final poem 'Balin and Balan' (written 1874, published 1885).[21]

These dates overlap with the explosion in visual representations of Arthurian material seen in the work of the Pre-Raphaelite Brotherhood – and not by coincidence. In 1857, publisher Edward Moxon issued a deluxe illustrated edition of Tennyson's poems (*figure 51*) which contained engravings by young artists such William Holman Hunt and Dante Gabriel Rossetti.[22] Many of the motifs featured in these illustrations would later go on to play central roles in

L

SPRING on the Polar Seas!—not violet-crowned
  By dewy Hours, nor to cærulean halls
Melodious hymned, yet Light itself around
  Her stately path, sheds starry coronals.
Sublime she comes, as when, from Dis set free,
Came, through the flash of Jove, Persephonè :

52 Written while the concept of natural selection was becoming an increasingly controversial subject, Edward Bulwer-Lytton's *King Arthur* (1853) features the hero journeying among the skeletons of dinosaurs, mammoths and what appear to be early hominids!

Oxford, Bodleian Library, 280 n.107, frontispiece.

these artists' major works. The connection between visual art and Arthurian literature would later be reinforced by Aubrey Beardsley's illustrations, published together with a modern-spelling reissue of Caxton's text by J.M. Dent in 1893–94.[23]

Although Tennyson's Arthurian poems were not explicitly directed at children, many of them were considered suitable reading for older boys and girls, and were used as school texts and recitations. In *Anne of Green Gables* (1908), L.M. Montgomery describes the experiences of the teenage heroine and her friends as they attempt to re-enact their reading of 'The Lady of Shalott' – with unexpectedly soggy consequences. Tennyson's Arthurian poems were seen as suitable for children in part due to their reproduction of motifs such as struggling to achieve glory through service, but also because of their self-conscious concern with morality. Tennyson himself, towards the end of his life, announced that his meaning was both instructive and spiritual, stating that 'I intended Arthur to represent the Ideal Soul of Man coming into contact with the warring elements of the flesh.'[24]

Just before Tennyson began work on his *Idylls*, Lord Edward Bulwer-Lytton was creating a very different Arthuriad: the twelve-book epic *King Arthur* (1848–49). The text refers to Arthur's story as that which is 'beloved as Fable, yet believed as Truth' – yet the story that it presents is distinctly unbelievable.[25] After winning his kingdom Arthur embarks upon a quest, travelling to, among other destinations, the Arctic Circle. He encounters trolls, polar bears and even 'the lurid skeletons of vanished races / They who, perchance ere man himself had birth / Ruled the moist slime of uncompleted earth' – in other words, dinosaurs! (*figure* 52).[26] Combining Arthurian material with elements drawn from Norse myth and classical literature, the poem legitimises the project of British conquest and imperialism via Merlin's prophecies of Arthur's empire, which will 'clasp a realm where never sets the sun'.[27] By demonstrating Arthur's dominance over the exotic and the monstrous, signified in terms of both geographical journeying and learning about newly discovered prehistoric creatures, the text manages to remain assured of the inevitability of English (and therefore British) superiority in the face of the new scientific discourses that were opening up at the time Lytton was writing.[28]

Boys' own Arthurs: adapting Malory for children

Tennyson's vision of chivalry – 'Live pure, speak true, right wrong, follow the King – / Else, wherefore born?' – had demonstrated that Arthurian literature could provide a valuable message for readers of all ages.[29] However, after the 1850s an increased demand arose for new versions of Malory's text written especially for children.[30] This impulse was partly moral (see below), but also based around Malory's use of 'antiquated spelling and quaint style', which was felt to be a hindrance to children's reading.[31] Frequently casting themselves as 'second Caxtons', redactors, abridgers and 'translators' of Malory sought to make these 'immortal' stories accessible, pleasurable and, above all, morally uplifting for a new generation.

The first of these was James Knowles, who explicitly announced his debt to Southey in his 1862 *The Story of King Arthur* (which was also dedicated, with the poet's permission, to Tennyson himself).[32] By redacting and updating the language of the text, Knowles hoped to 'place it in boys' libraries anywhere beside "Robinson Crusoe" and "The Arabian Nights"', but also to modify it 'where changed manners and morals have made it absolutely necessary to do so for the preservation of a lofty original ideal'.[33] The sense of Arthurian literature as a morally uplifting 'guide-book' for young readers was further reinforced by Sidney Lanier, whose 1880 *The Boy's King Arthur* provided a richly illustrated and visually seductive portrait of the glories of Arthurian life. Lanier urged his child readers – here, again, specifically gendered as *boy* readers – to join the 'fine fellowship … of lordly Sir Launcelot, of generous Sir Tristram, of stainless Sir Galahad … as well, alas! as … of cowardly King Mark, of traitorous Sir Mordred, and of wicked Morgan le Fay'.[34] This catalogue of virtuous knights, each identified with a trait that the reader should seek to emulate, coupled with a matching list of villains and their besetting sins, is a straightforward extension of Caxton's plea to the reader to 'doo after the good and leve the evyl'. Given that Lanier's edition was reprinted as recently as 2006, it appears that this invitation has been, at least to some extent, taken up by successive generations of readers.[35]

The popularity of knighthood and chivalry also infiltrated other, non-Arthurian texts, particularly those concerned with conduct. Thomas Hughes's *Tom Brown's School Days* (1857), for example, focuses on the daily struggles of boys at an English public school – yet while 'the language of chivalry never obtrudes into the cheerful mixture of slang and breeziness in which the book is written', the themes of brotherhood, fellowship and striving to do right strongly reflect the drives of Tennyson's medievalism.[36] Arthur Hughes's pictures for the 1869 illustrated edition further reinforce this – for example, in a scene where Tom struggles with his personal vice of 'cribbing', or using copy-notes, he is depicted as a young knight at prayer, while the leading illustration to chapter

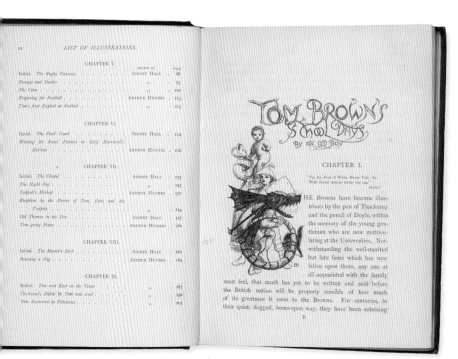

TOM. BROWN'S
School Days
By AN OLD BOY

CHAPTER I.

The Poet of White Horse Vale, Sir,
With liberal notions under your cap.
                                    Ballad.

HE Browns have become illustrious by the pen of Thackeray and the pencil of Doyle, within the memory of the young gentlemen who are now matriculating at the Universities. Notwithstanding the well-merited but late fame which has now fallen upon them, any one at all acquainted with the family must feel, that much has yet to be written and said before the British nation will be properly sensible of how much of its greatness it owes to the Browns. For centuries, in their quiet, dogged, home-spun way, they have been subduing

B

53 The illustrations to the 1869 edition of *Tom Brown's Schooldays* repeatedly evoke the image of the young hero as a knight – here, he appears as a very young child watching a re-enactment of the story of 'St George and the Dragon'.

Oxford, Bodleian Library, 205 e.47 sig B, p. xx.

1 features the infant Tom being held up to witness a re-enactment of the legend of St George (*figure 53*).

Arthurian influence was also apparent in the non-Arthurian works of late-Victorian authors such as George MacDonald and William Morris. *The Well at the World's End*, while not explicitly Arthurian, draws thematic elements such as the quest-narrative from both Victorian retellings of Malory and Morris's own position as a member of the Pre-Raphaelite Brotherhood – he had earlier published a volume of adult poetry entitled *The Defence of Guenevere*.[37] MacDonald's fantasy novels also mix elements of folk tale and fairy tale with highly coloured images of quest and knighthood. Both of these authors provided major sources of inspiration for C.S. Lewis and J.R.R. Tolkien. Lewis, in particular, regarded MacDonald's *Phantastes* (1894), which references the adventures of Galahad and Perceval, as a formative influence, as described in Chapter 3 above.[38] He also named one of the locations in his late-Victorian-children's-literature pastiche *The Magician's Nephew* 'the wood between the worlds', presumably in homage to Morris.[39]

The tradition of Tom Thumb as an Arthurian hero was also briefly revived by Charlotte Yonge in *The History of the Life and Death of the Good Knight Sir Thomas Thumb* (1885). Yonge was already familiar with Arthurian themes after using the figure of Galahad as a point of comparison for the hero in her novel *The Heir of Redclyffe* (1853). In *Tom Thumb*, she combines references to Geoffrey of Monmouth, the Stanzaic *Morte Arthur*, Spenser,

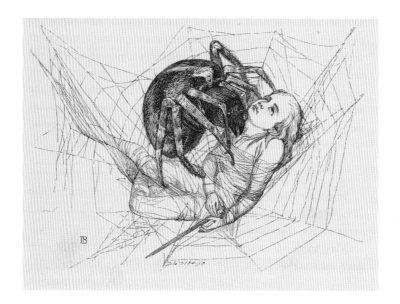

54 In 1855, Charlotte Yonge revived the connection between the figure of Tom Thumb and the Arthurian legends. Here, her Tom fights to defend Arthur's empty throne from the spiders who have overtaken the castle. Illustration by Jemima Blackburn.

Shakespeare and Tennyson.[40] In Yonge's story, Tom forsakes Arthur's court for the world of the fairies, led into temptation by the deceitful Puck. However, he later repents and returns to fulfil his duty as a knight – only to find that Arthur and his court have perished at the hands of Mordred in his absence. Undaunted, Tom dies fighting off the spiders that are attempting to weave webs around Arthur's empty throne, and achieves the ultimate glory – 'honourable death as a Christian'[41] (*figure* 54).

Cleaning up Camelot

The problem still remained, however, of how to handle the more sexually and morally difficult elements of the text. If parents and teachers were content to have their charges read about the adventures of Arthur's knights 'fighting for the blameless king', 'the evil work of Lancelot and the Queen' remained a different matter.[42] The late nineteenth and early twentieth centuries saw a rise in bowdlerised adaptations which sought to provide a view of the medieval past as 'pre-adult … hyper-moralized and asexual', moving from Malory's and Tennyson's compromised yet sympathetic sinners to a set of knights that could be presented as suitable role models for Victorian and Edwardian boys and girls.[43] A late and particularly egregious example was written by Roma White, writing under the pseudonym 'Blanche Winder', in 1925.[44] Drawing upon Geoffrey of Monmouth, Chrétien, the Vulgate Cycle and the *Mabinogion*, as well as upon Malory, she infantilises scenes and characters almost beyond recognition, replacing magic with whimsy and leaving so many gaps that the story ceases to make sense. Merlin, who in Geoffrey's text is fathered by an incubus and in Malory's identified as 'a devyls son', is here a 'little fairy baby' who, when christened, 'laughed and shouted with gladness, and clapped his wee white hands [saying] 'I am a human baby now!'[45] Uther becomes a 'good king' who *rescues* Ygierne rather than killing her husband, and Lancelot is 'the little prince of the Lake' whose devotion to Guinevere remains entirely chaste.[46]

A more nuanced adaptation is Leonora and Andrew Lang's 1902 *Book of Romance*, which combines selected stories from Malory and other medieval traditions such as the Robin Hood ballads, the *Chanson de Roland* and the Icelandic saga of Grettir the Strong (*figure* 55). In this version, Lancelot is sent to collect Guinevere from her father's house prior to her marriage to Arthur – thus, importantly, they fall in love before it is technically adulterous for them to do so.[47] By subtly alluding to emotional infidelity while never explicitly sexualising the characters, the text creates an acceptable Edwardian Arthuriad 'without quite losing Malory's effect'.[48]

For the American children's market, Howard Pyle commenced work on his Arthurian retellings (*figure* 56) – based on both Malory and his own invention – with *The Story of King Arthur and*

55 One of the more nuanced Edwardian adaptations of Malory for children, Leonora and Andrew Lang's *Book of Romance* (1902) refers to the adulterous relationship between Lancelot and Guinevere, carefully presented in terms of emotional, rather than sexual, infidelity.

Oxford, Bodleian Library, Johnson e.3694, illustration facing p. 132.

How Arthur drew forth ye Sword.

Chapter Third.

How Several Kings and High Dukes Assayed to Draw the Sword Out of the Anvil and How They Failed. Likewise How Arthur Made the Assay and Succeeded Therein.

SO when the morning of Christmas day had come, many thousands of folk of all qualities, both gentle and simple, gathered together in front of the cathedral for to behold the assay of that sword.

Now there had been a canopy of embroidered cloth of divers colors spread above the sword and the anvil, and a platform had been built around about the cube of marble stone. And nigh unto that place there had been a throne for the Archbishop established; for the Archbishop was to overlook that assay and to see that every circumstance was fulfilled with due equity and circumspection.

So, when the morning was half gone by, the Archbishop himself came with great pomp of estate and took his seat upon the high throne that had been placed for him, and all his court of clerks and knights gathered about him, so that he presented a very proud and excellent appearance of courtliness.

Now unto that assay there had gathered nineteen kings and sixteen dukes, and each of these was of such noble and exalted estate that he entertained high hopes that he would that day be approved before the world to be the right king and overlord of all Britain. Wherefore after the Archbishop had established himself upon his throne, there came several of these and made demand that he should straightway put that matter to the test. So the Archbishop commanded his herald for to sound a trumpet, and to bid all who had the right to make assay of the sword to come unto that adventure, and the herald did according as the Archbishop ordered.

And when the herald had sounded his trumpet there immediately appeared the first of those kings to make trial of the sword, and he who came was King Lot of Orkney and the Isles. With King Lot there came eleven

---

56 Howard Pyle's Arthurian adaptations recast the stories for the American market, providing additional Christian emphasis and moral weight as well as stressing the achievement of the knights as individuals.

Howard Pyle, *The Story of King Arthur and His Knights* (1903), 'How Arthur drew forth ye Sword'. Oxford, Bodleian Library, 2543 d.8, p. 28.

His Knights (1903), later joined by *The Story of the Champions of the Round Table* (1905), *The Story of Sir Launcelot and His Companions* (1907) and *The Story of the Grail and the Passing of Arthur* (1910). Following on from his earlier work on *The Merry Adventures of Robin Hood* (1883) Pyle sought both to capitalise on existing interest in children's medievalism and to give Arthur's knights additional moral weight and individualism. For example, in a scene in which Malory's Launcelot is chastened for his sinfulness during the Grail quest, Pyle's Launcelot is given both a reassurance of God's forgiveness and a lecture on the importance of not giving in to the sin of despair: 'For every man may sin,' he is told, 'and yet again may sin; yet still is he God's handiwork, and still God is near by His handiwork to aid him ever to a fresh endeavour to righteousness.'[49]

It is worth noting that these idealised and hyper-moralised versions of Arthur and the Middle Ages were also questioned, parodied and undercut during this period. Most famously, Mark Twain's initially serialised *A Connecticut Yankee in King Arthur's Court* (November 1889–April 1890) presents the knights of Arthur's court as backward, gullible and in need of the guidance of a nineteenth-century hero. As described above (p. 85), E. Nesbit's *Five Children and It* (1902) also pokes fun at the romanticisation of the Middle Ages. Beardsley's illustrations, while intended for

57 Aubrey Beardsley's Aesthetic-style illustrations, produced for J.M. Dent's luxury edition of Caxton's *Morte Darthur* in 1893, share visual elements with the Pre-Raphaelite images yet at times appear almost to mock Victorian conventions associating Arthurian literature with sexual purity, staunch masculinity and moral uprightness.

Oxford, Bodleian Library, Vet. 2543 d.56, Vol. 2, pp. 760–61.

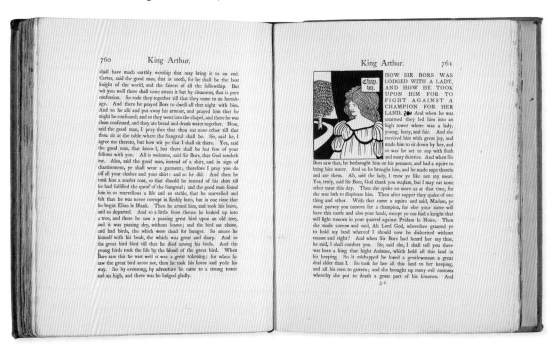

an adult audience, can also be seen as a critical commentary on the perception of Arthur's court as a site of ideal masculinity through their depiction of overpowering villainesses and oddly static, passive and androgynous knights (*figure 57*).

Arthur joins the Boy Scouts

The influence of Arthur and his knights as a spur to good conduct for boys soon spread beyond the confines of fiction, as the proprietors of the many Church-affiliated and free-standing 'boys' clubs' sought to find ways to motivate young men to behave in socially desirable ways. One of the earliest of these was in fact not Baden-Powell's Scouts, but William Byron Forbush's US-based 'Knights of King Arthur', from whom Baden-Powell drew significant inspiration. Forbush's approach, as laid out in his 1901 social study *The Boy Problem*, was designed both to curb the behaviour of the overly boisterous and to provide an incentive for the more sheltered boys to 'rise above all that is weak and effeminate'.[50] Founded in Massachusetts in 1893, the group numbered 130,000 members in 1922.[51] Each chapter of the club, known as a 'Castle', consisted of boys aged from 12 to 18, led by an adult, known as 'the Merlin'. Each member would choose the name of one of Arthur's knights, and would progress through the ranks of Page, Esquire and, finally, Knight.[52] Meetings were dominated by sporting contests, informal talks and the planning and implementation of 'quests' to perform good deeds or athletic feats.

Similarly drawing upon Arthurian imagery, although with very different political intentions, George Herbert Whyte, a member of the London Theosophical Society, launched two children's clubs in 1908, 'The Knights of the Round Table' and its junior branch 'The Golden Chain'. At the meetings of these clubs, children of Society members were instructed in moral behaviour, medieval history and the Theosophists' mixture of Christian and Eastern spirituality. They were supported by *The Lotus Journal*, a Theosophist children's magazine which ran from 1903 to 1912 and provided members with information and inspirational stories, drawing on Tennyson's *Idylls* and heraldic manuals as well as the teachings of the Society.[53] The Knights of the Round Table remains active today, and continues to run youth camps and activities based around the themes of spirituality and personal development.[54]

Arthur at war

As historian Mark Girouard suggests, World War I represented the coming to fruition of the Victorian and Edwardian obsession with chivalry:

> all those who had been at public schools knew exactly what was expected of them. But so … did all Boy Scouts, past and present, all Cadets, all members of boys' clubs and boys' brigades, all readers of the right adventure stories in the right magazines.[55]

Although St George featured heavily in the iconography of recruitment for the British and Allied forces, the Arthurian

58 'How Mordred was slain by Arthur, and how by him Arthur was hurt to the death'. Produced in 1917 for Alfred Pollard's adaptation of Malory, Arthur Rackham's bleak portrait of mutual destruction provides a disturbing visual echo of the blasted landscape of the trenches.

Alfred Pollard, illustrated by Arthur Rackham, *The Romance of King Arthur and His Knights of the Round Table* (1917). Oxford, Bodleian Library, 2543 e.38, illustration facing p. 486.

legends also had a significant part to play. In the USA, Lanier's *The Boy's King Arthur* was given a timely reissue in 1917 with new illustrations by N.C. Wyeth, and was reprinted again with the original Alfred Kappes illustrations in 1920.[56] In Britain, Baden-Powell published *Young Knights of the Empire* in 1916,[57] while Alfred Pollard's *The Romance of King Arthur and His Knights of the Round Table* (1917) presented a new adaptation of Malory. However, it also became increasingly difficult to present images of battle and conflict in an uncomplicatedly positive light. In Pollard's edition, Arthur Rackham's illustration of the final battle between Arthur and Mordred seems to give an unsettling visual echo of a landscape distorted by trench warfare (*figure* 58). British recruiting posters also often drew upon Victorian-style chivalric imagery, although typically featuring St George rather than King Arthur, echoing the juxtaposition of the two heroes in Baden-Powell's *Yarns for Boy Scouts*.[58]

The iconography of the immediate post-war period also reflected the ways in which the men who survived the conflict had been taught to think about chivalry in boyhood. The World War I memorial window in Oxford's Church of St Michael at the North Gate, for example, features a victorious St George standing over the slain dragon (*figure* 59), while the Great War memorial windows at Bristol's Clifton College specifically reference both Galahad and Arthur.[59]

After the memorialisation of the 'war to end all wars' had settled, the 1920s saw a downturn in literary depictions of Arthur and his knights, T.S. Eliot's oblique Arthurian references in *The Waste Land* (1922) aside. This was reversed by the publication of T.H. White's extraordinary Arthurian tetralogy *The Once and Future King*, beginning with *The Sword in the Stone* in 1938. The story follows 'the Wart', an (apparently) orphan boy who is tutored by the absent-minded Merlin the magician, and who eventually goes on to pull the fabled sword from the stone to become King of All England. The book was followed by the less popular and more adult-oriented *The Witch in the Wood* (1938), *The Ill-Made Knight* (1940) and *The Candle in the Wind* (1958). A final text, *The Book of Merlyn*, was published after White's death in 1977. Throughout the series, but particularly in the first book, White populates his Camelot with anachronisms that are often slyly satirical jabs at the interwar English upper classes: Merlin presents his teaching credentials from Aristotle, Hecate and the Master of Trinity College, the Wart's guardian Sir Ector quaffs port and discusses 'giant-huntin'' in the manner of a 1920s' Master of Fox Hounds, and knights accuse one another of cheating at jousting by crying 'Swindler!' and 'Beastly bully!'[60] The truly original aspect of White's Arthurian writing, however, is his attitude to warfare. Merlin's quest, which later becomes Arthur's, is not to achieve moral purity, nor to attain dominance through the creation of an empire – it is to establish a world in which 'Might' does not dominate over 'Right'. Writing on the eve of,

59 World War I memorial window, Church of St Michael at the North Gate, Oxford. After the war, images of knighthood – and particularly of Arthur, Galahad and St George – were frequently drawn upon for the creation of memorial statues, windows and other commemorations.

By kind permission of the Church of St Michael at the North Gate. Photograph by Nick Cistone.

into and beyond World War II, White's fraught relationship with the question of pacifism versus nationalism is never truly resolved: his Arthur cannot avert the Battle of Camlann and *The Candle in the Wind* concludes with the old king walking calmly towards his death.

The shadow of World War II falls even more clearly on the British Arthurian literature produced in the second half of the twentieth century. Both C.S. Lewis and J.R.R. Tolkien worked closely with Arthurian texts, and while Lewis is better known for his children's series *The Chronicles of Narnia*, the more adult-oriented *That Hideous Strength* (1945) features a band of Christians led by 'the Pendragon', who must call on the aid of Merlin (buried for a thousand years beneath the grounds of the local university) in order to defeat an evil government conspiracy.[61] The modernity, technology and social reorganisation accelerated by the war effort, depicted most clearly in Lewis's terrifying N.I.C.E (National Institution for Co-ordinated Experiments) is contrasted negatively with the Christian spirituality, comforting (to Lewis) social and gender hierarchies, and sense of romance that the author associates with the Arthurian past.

In 1934, the discovery of the long-lost Winchester Manuscript by Walter Oakeshott reinvigorated both academic and literary interest in Malory's *Le Morte Darthur*. However, Eugène Vinaver's edition of the new text was not published until 1947.[62] The first children's author to respond to this new development was Roger Lancelyn Green, a friend of Lewis's and a member of the 'Inklings', the group of Oxford writers centred on Lewis and Tolkien. Appearing in 1953, Green's *King Arthur and His Knights of the Round Table* adopts Vinaver's model of 'quite separate stories' rather than a single overarching narrative, providing 'a certain coherence, but no fixed plan'.[63] Perhaps most interestingly, Green's retelling also shifts the emphasis of many of Arthur's early battles – rather than defeating rebel British kings or striving for perfection in holy quests, much of Green's Arthur's energy is devoted to the defeat of 'the Saxons, who could never ... be contented with their savage, unfruitful homes in Germany' and instead 'come stealing across the North Sea in their long ships, to kill or drive out the Britons and settle in their homes' – a telling refocusing of the story in the days following World War II.[64] Similarly, Susan Cooper, author of the Arthurian-inflected *The Dark Is Rising* series (1965–77), acknowledges that 'the struggle between the Light and the Dark in my books has ... to do with the fact that when I was four World War II broke out.'[65] She adds that 'the experience of having people drop bombs on your head ... led to a very strong sense of Us and Them. Of course Us is always the good, and Them is always the bad.'[66]

In the United States, Vinaver's edition sparked the interest of novelist John Steinbeck, who in 1956 began a never-to-be-finished modern-English translation of Malory's text.[67] In his draft Preface, Steinbeck uses his own version of Malory's fifteenth-century English to relate his experiences as an imaginative 9-year-old reader of the *Morte Darthur*. When the child Steinbeck played at being a knight, 'yit chaunced that squyre lyke dutyes fell to my systir of / vi wyntre age that for jantyl prouesse had no felawe lyvynge' (it chanced that squire-like duties fell to my sister of / six years, who for gentle prowess had no peer living). However, the adult Steinbeck admitted that

> Yt haps somtymes in saddnesse and pytie that who faithful servys / ys not faithful sene so my fayre and sikker systir squyre dures yet undubbed / Wherefore thys daye I mak amendys to by power and rayse hir knyghte and gyff hir loudis / And fro thys hower she shall be hyght Syr Mayrie Stynbec of the Vayle Salynis / God gyve hir worshypp saunz jaupardye.
>
> (It sometimes happens in sadness and pity that faithful service is not appreciated, so my fair and loyal sister remained unrecognised as a squire. / Wherefore this day I make amends within my power and raise her to knighthood and give her praise. / And from this hour she shall be called Sir Marie Steinbeck of Salinas Valley. / God give her worship without peril.)[68]

This story provides an endearing glimpse of the ways in which early-twentieth-century children were investing themselves in the Arthurian legend – and, moreover, Steinbeck's account of his sister Mary's role suggests that this imaginative engagement was not solely the preserve of boys.

Both Cooper and Alan Garner (*The Weirdstone of Brisingamen*, 1960); *The Moon of Gomrath*, 1963) drew on Arthurian elements, but did not exclusively rely upon them, creating children's fantasies which blended Arthurian, Norse and Welsh mythology.[69] Garner opens *The Weirdstone of Brisingamen* with the image

60 The opening section of Alan Garner's *The Weirdstone of Brisingamen* draws on the question of whether or not Arthur remains dead after the destruction of his kingdom. (*left*) A handwritten transcription of sections of both Malory's conclusion and Caxton's epigraph to Malory's text, found in Garner's rough notes for the book. (*right*) An extract from the Arthurian episode in the author's handwritten copy of the text.

Oxford, Bodleian Library, Alan Garner Collection (BYU), Box 10, Folder 3, notes. © Alan Garner; Oxford, Bodleian Library, Alan Garner Collection (BYU), Box 10, Folder 5, p. 3. © Alan Garner.

The wizard, for such he was, commanded the farmer to rise. "I promise you safe conduct," he said. "Do not be afraid; for living wonders you shall see here."

Beyond the rock stood a pair of iron gates. These the wizard opened, & ushered the farmer & his horse down a narrow tunnel deep into the hill. A light, subdued but beautiful, marked their way. The passage ended, & they stepped into a cave, & there a wondrous sight met the farmer's eyes —— a hundred & forty knights in in silver armour, & by the side of all but one a milk

they lie in enchanted sleep," said
a day will come — & come it will
be in direst peril, & England's
out from the hill these must
thrice lost, thrice won, upon the
emy into the sea."

mer; dumb with awe, turned with
urther cavern, & here mounds of
ous stones lay strewn along the ground
that you can carry in payment for

the farmer had crammed his
lands.'], his shirt, & his fists with
hurried him up the long tunnel
the gates. The farmer stumbled,
rolled, he looked, there was

!CAR, GAD,
OLIVER & BOYD. FEB '29   A. CARMICHAEL.

And for to passe the tyme thys book shal be plesaunte to rede in, but for to gyve fayth & byleve that al is trewe that is conteyned herein, ye be at your lyberté.

William Caxton: 31 July 1485.

Yet som men say in many p[art]ys of Inglonde that kynge Arthur ys nat dede, but h[ad] by the wyll of oure lorde Jesu into another place; & men say that he shall com agayne, & he shall wynne the Holy Crosse. Yet I wolt nat say that hit shall be so, but rather I wolde sey: here in thys worlde he chaunged hys lyff. And many men say that there ys wryjten uppon the tumbe thys:

HIC IACET ARTHURUS, REX QUONDAM REXQUE FUTURUS.

And for to passe the tyme thys book shal be plesaunte to rede in, but for to gyve fayth and byleve that al is trewe that is conteyned herein, ye be at your lyberté.

HIC · IACET · ARTHURUS ·
REX · QUONDAM · ATQ^u ·
+ FUTURUS +

of the Sleepers, men in armour who lie in an enchanted sleep beneath Alderley Edge 'until the day will come – and come it will – when England shall be in direst peril'.[70] Although the Sleepers are never specifically linked with Arthur, just as the wizard Cadellin is never specifically referenced as Merlin, these figures are drawn in part from Malory's equivocation surrounding the final fate of Arthur: Garner's notes for the book include a transcription of Malory's conclusion and Caxton's epilogue to *Le Morte Darthur* (*figure* 60). It is interesting to note that both Garner and Lewis make use of the image of Arthurian figures who sleep under the earth and will return in a moment of particular national crisis: Lewis also briefly re-references the trope in *The Voyage of the Dawn Treader*, where he suggests that the children's return to Narnia is 'as if King Arthur came back to Britain, as some people say he will… And I say the sooner the better.'[71] However, Garner is also working here with traditional Cheshire folklore: the legend of 'Arthur and his warriors who would not awaken until George, son of George, was king'[72] has long existed in the area independently of Malory or other medieval storytellers.

Reinventing Arthur

The second half of the twentieth century and the beginning of the twenty-first have seen an explosion in the popularity of Arthurian retellings for children and adults. To cover even a small proportion of these would take an entire book – and indeed, several of these have already been written (see Further Reading). For the remainder of this chapter, I will focus on Arthurian children's literature that seeks not to retell the received stories of Arthur and his knights, but to revise or reinvent them. These reinvents are frequently characterised by an antagonistic or oppositional re-imagining of the story, and are often intended to reach out to an audience that has not traditionally engaged with Arthurian literature. While traditional literary retellings such as Rosemary Sutcliffe's *The Sword and the Circle*, *The Light Beyond the Forest* and *The Road to Camlann*, Neil Philip's *The Tale of Sir Gawain* and Kevin Crossley-Holland's 'Arthur Trilogy' and *Gatty's Tale* have continued to be read and enjoyed by successive generations of readers, these reinventions also have a fascinating place in the continuation of Arthurian writing.[73]

As Michael Torregrossa points out, the influence of Arthurian literature on comics – and, indeed, the influence of comics on writers of Arthurian literature – has been 'largely neglected or ignored by Arthurian scholars'.[74] However, 'the adventures of the four-color king'[75] are responsible for a significant proportion of Arthurian literature's continued popularity. Running continuously for over seventy years, Harold Foster's *Prince Valiant in the Days of King Arthur* (first appearance 1937; with collaborator John Cullen Murphy from 1970, aided by his son and daughter from 1979; Gary Gianni took over in 2004) is one of the longest-running newspaper strips in existence. Like a Victorian Arthuriad or a Scouting

manual, the strip's earlier adventures stress the importance of young Valiant's attempts to prove his virtue and prowess in order to be admitted to Arthur's court, while later numbers follow his struggles as a patriarch to protect his kingdom and family. The series has also spawned multiple published collections, two feature films and a children's animated series.[76]

In the UK, Marvel Comics' *Captain Britain* (first appearance 1976) featured the combination of contemporary protagonist and Arthurian setting also seen in the work of more conventional novelists such as Lewis, Williams, Cooper and Garner (*figure 61*).[77] Young physics student Brian Braddock stumbles into a stone circle and is presented with a choice between the 'Amulet of Right' and 'The Sword of Might' (echoing White's division between 'Might' and 'Right' in *The Once and Future King*). Choosing the amulet, Brian is transformed by Merlin into the titular superhero, and battles foes such as 'Modred the Evil' and the ghostly 'White Rider'. A 1990s' series reboot saw a new version of Brian choose both the amulet *and* the sword in order to become the reincarnation of Arthur himself. A further reinvention is seen in the dystopian *Camelot 3000* (1982–85), in which the far future sees Arthur awoken and his knights reincarnated in various parts of the world.[78] Casting Gawain as a black South African businessman, Guinevere as a female US Army officer and, interestingly, Tristram as a woman who remains in love with the female Isolde despite her change in gender, the story plays with sexuality and identity in challenging and fascinating ways as the

61 Marvel Comics' *Captain Britain* drew heavily on Arthurian images and themes. In this early scene, Merlin and his daughter offer the hero a choice between the Amulet of Right and the Sword of Might in order to enable him to take over Arthur's role as protector of Britain.

Page 18 from *Captain Britain Summer Special 1979*: Merlin offers Brian the choice of sword or amulet. Oxford, Bodleian Library, Per. 254399 d.119. © and TM Marvel and subs.

reunited company struggles to save the world from aliens sent by the time-travelling Morgan le Fay.

Marion Zimmer Bradley's New Age Feminist *The Mists of Avalon* (1983) rewrote the story from the perspective of Morgan le Fay, a villainous figure since at least the time of Malory.[79] A more specifically child-oriented regendering of the Middle Ages also appears in the works of Tamora Pierce. While Pierce's novels are not overtly Arthurian, her first series *The Song of the Lioness* (1983–88) borrows an important element from Malory's 'Tale of Sir Gareth'. This is the theme of the *bel inconnu*, the 'fair unknown' or disguised noble boy who is mistaken for a weakling until his true identity is revealed when he performs deeds of greatness.[80] Pierce's *bel inconnu* is Alanna, a girl whose gender prevents those around her from realising her potential as a warrior until she disguises herself in order to train as a knight – and proceeds to triumph over her male adversaries and competitors in an unabashed moment of 1980s' liberal feminist wish-fulfilment. Pierce cites Pyle as one of her major early influences, and while Alanna's model of empowerment through individual self-advancement appears closely drawn from Pyle's presentation of knighthood as an individualist triumph, Pierce's later novels move away from this towards a moral schema which draws more heavily on collectivist politics.[81] Echoes of the *bel inconnu* can also be seen in the rejected and abused figure of the pre-Hogwarts Harry in J.K. Rowling's *Harry Potter and the Philosopher's Stone* (1997). Rowling's use of the drawing of the 'Sword of Gryffindor' as a plot device in both *Harry Potter and the*

Chamber of Secrets (1998) and *Harry Potter and the Deathly Hallows* (2007) also echoes the central importance of sword-drawing in Malory and some of his French sources (as well as in T.H. White and twentieth-century Arthurian film adaptations).

Three more young-adult-oriented reimaginings of Arthurian literature are Mary Stewart's *The Wicked Day* (1983), Nancy Springer's *I Am Mordred* (1998) and Meg Cabot's *Avalon High* (2005).[82] Stewart's and Springer's texts concern Mordred, while Cabot's story is narrated from the perspective of Ellie Harrison, the character corresponding to Elaine of Astolat in the text's modern-day American setting. They are drawn from separate traditions, with Springer's and Stewart's texts specifically referencing Malory while each chapter of Cabot's is prefaced with a quotation from Tennyson's *The Lady of Shalott*. All three struggle with the question of 'destiny' and whether predestination – in the form of the traditional outcome of the Arthurian story – can be overcome. In particular, Springer's text divides its sympathies between the forlorn figure of Arthur, condemned to child murder by his incestuous union with Morgause, and the narrator Mordred, cursed with foreknowledge, who 'grieve[s] because [he] know[s] how the song must end'.[83] The theme of multiple perspectives and misunderstanding is also touched upon in Peter Dickinson's *Merlin Dreams* (1988), which sympathetically rewrites the figure of Nimue 'the damesell of the lake' as acting with Merlin's blessing and collaboration in placing him within the earth, rather than maliciously seeking to trap him, and

Philip Reeve's *Here Lies Arthur* (2007), which focuses on the ways in which storytelling can be used in the service of political and social misdirection.[84]

The continuing importance of Arthurian stories as a cultural touchstone became apparent once more in 2008, when BBC 1 broadcast the first episode of *Merlin*, a new family television drama purporting to follow the adventures of the young wizard and his friends.[85] Outrage followed from many quarters regarding the 'politically correct' changes that the show's producers had made to what audiences perceived as 'the traditional British legends' – among these, altering the ages of the protagonists to make Merlin and Arthur contemporaries, casting Guinevere as a servant rather than a princess, and hiring Angel Coulby, a woman of Afro-Caribbean descent, to play her. Yet this text, too, makes both old and new uses of the Arthurian story: in addition to its explorations of race and class, it uses the growing friendship between the arrogant Prince Arthur and the quiet, bookish and under-confident Merlin as a site for comparing and negotiating multiple forms of masculinity in the twenty-first century – a negotiation that goes back to the contrasts seen between these figures in Malory's work, if not before.

Conclusion

As this brief survey has suggested, the figures of Arthur and his Knights of the Round Table can be remodelled to suit the purposes of each successive generation of readers and writers. Whether acting as a reference point for heroism in the seventh-century *Y Gododdin*, providing a guide to noble conduct for Caxton's London readers in 1485 or serving as Baden-Powell's exemplar for the building of a strong empire in 1908, Arthurian literature models adult expectations regarding behaviour and conduct for young readers – but there is great variation from period to period about what this behaviour should be.

Moreover, while the stories have often been framed as ideal texts for children, dissenting voices such as Ascham's, and the drive towards bowdlerisation in Victorian and Edwardian children's literature, suggest that the sexual and relationship-driven aspects of the stories have often been seen as unsuitable for young readers. In the twentieth century, Cooper, Lewis and Green saw Arthurian literature as a way of framing global politics as conflicts between 'Dark and Light', 'Them and Us' – but White's Arthuriad stressed the futility of national conflict and the importance of peace. Moreover, re-imaginings such as those of Stewart, Springer, Dickinson and Reeve suggest that any 'Them' is also potentially an 'Us': that there are two sides to every story. Ultimately, it appears that the most important role of Arthur and his court in literature for children is to remain malleable, able to stand in for whatever the author and his or her society perceive to be ideal – as Lytton would have it, 'Beloved as Fable' yet also, in some important symbolic ways, 'believed as Truth'.

5

The magic of finger and thumb: early movable books for children

HANNAH FIELD

REVIOUS chapters have considered magic and myth as themes in or inspirations for children's books. This chapter treats the uses of magic in a different, but no less established, branch of children's publishing: innovations of format and design in popular children's literature from the eighteenth century onward. Books that are here referred to as movable books but which encompass examples that might more properly be called novelty books will be examined in terms of their unique appropriation of magical and folkloric content.[1] Hence the focus shifts somewhat, to emphasise the material properties of children's books. This chapter is also a departure in its discussion of books intended for younger readers, and books that are by and large out of print. Examining such works showcases the Bodleian's impressive holdings of rare children's books, a key component of which is the Opie Collection of Children's Literature. The personal collection of Iona and Peter Opie, eminent folklorists and scholars of children's literature, the

Opie Collection – containing 20,000 or so volumes – was acquired by the Bodleian in 1988 after a public fund-raising appeal, Iona Opie donating half the value of the collection. It is well catalogued, and now accessible on microfiche as well as in the original.

Children's literature is by no means the only place in which movable books have flourished. Indeed, movable parts have been added to books for quite some time. Peter Apian's resplendent *Astronomicum Caesareum* (1540) used rotating discs or volvelles to demonstrate the movements of celestial objects, providing a sort of companion to the astrolabe. Another celebrated sixteenth-century example, Vesalius's *De humani corporis fabrica librorum epitome* (1543), encouraged the reader to assemble complex layered models of the human body from its anatomical plates. Ramón Llull's philosophical volvelles were centuries earlier even than either of these, his *Ars Magna* appearing in 1305.[2] (Llull – as Ramon Lully – appears in John Masefield's beloved children's novel *The Box of Delights*, first published in 1935.) Such authors used movable mechanisms to explain, mimic or speculate on the natural world through the book. More recently, movable parts in books have often been associated with a different context: the children's book.

Brian Alderson has observed:

the establishment of [children's literature] as a self-sufficient department of the book-trade took place in the second half of the eighteenth century – while the years of wide and varied progress (when the so-called 'classic texts' arrived) were those of the mid-nineteenth century.[3]

Part of what happened during these centuries was the diversification of publishers' wares. Movable books for children comprise a vast range of formats, from flat, simple paper objects like harlequinades and concertina-folded panoramas, to three-dimensional mechanical experiments in the book, like the pop-up. Across these formats, and from their inception into the present day, children's movables frequently deal with magic. Rather than offering an exhaustive survey of movables (which has already been provided in a number of admirable bibliographies), this chapter discusses in detail the uses of magical content in five movables for children, from the eighteenth and nineteenth centuries, and largely drawn from the Opie Collection. Movables tend to co-opt the child's popular enthusiasm for fantasy to their own purposes, using magic and enchantment both as diverting narrative content and as an explanation for the movable's unique properties as a material book. Hence whether the book's magic entails metamorphoses, magic tricks or content such as nursery rhymes, fairy tales or fairies and Fairyland, the enchantment of children's movables resides in the physical book as an object as much as what the text contains.

Magical metamorphoses

The first movables associated with the juvenile market are the eighteenth-century flap books referred to as harlequinades. The harlequinade is a small book, in shape and size like a pamphlet. It typically comprises four panels, each overlaid with two flaps.

Hence any individual panel of the harlequinade contains three different images depending on whether one, both or neither of the flaps is lifted. The reader turns a flap up or down (hence the alternative term 'turn-up') at the salient moment in the story to reveal a new image and block of text. Robert Sayer, a London print, map and chart publisher, is credited as the originator of the form, although earlier manuscript examples using a similar structure survive.[4] The Bodleian holds a number of Sayer titles, as well as eighteenth-century harlequinades from other publishers, such as the Tringhams, and some uncut harlequinade sheets produced early in the nineteenth century. These last acquisitions demonstrate how the harlequinade is made better than any verbal description: beautifully digitised, they are available online as part of the electronic archive of the John Johnson Collection of Printed Ephemera.[5]

Harlequinades are theatrical movables, summarising the plots of contemporary performances in short rhyming verses and sometimes listing the specific theatres from which they originate. (Like the nineteenth-century sheets for the juvenile theatre remembered fondly by figures including Charles Dickens and Robert Louis Stevenson, they sold either plain or coloured at different price points.[6]) The harlequinade comes from the theatrical interlude of the same name: the section in the eighteenth-century English pantomime in which Harlequin and a number of other characters lifted from the *commedia dell'arte* tradition capered and chased each other around the stage. These books reference Harlequin from their very titles onwards, as in the case of, for instance, the Bodleian examples *Harlequin's Invasion* (1770), *Harlequin Cherokee or the Indian Chiefs in London* (1772), *Harlequin Skeleton* (1772) and *Robinson Crusoe or Harlequin Friday* (1781), and there are many others of a similar kind.[7] Harlequin's attribute in the on-stage harlequinades was a magical bat or sword (a continuation of the *batacchio* or slapstick of the *commedia*), a prop that the harlequin-ade books deploy to excellent effect.

Harlequin Skeleton, a famous example published by Sayer, illuminates the way this works (*figure 62*). Harlequin disguises himself as a skeleton to woo his Columbine in the house of her father, an anatomist. The early part of the story shows the dis-guised Harlequin frightening the Clown, Harlequin's traditional opponent – here the anatomist's credulous manservant – who believes the skeleton to be 'Death a-dancing'. The movable flaps give the harlequinade's short narrative much, if not all, of its dramatic purchase. In panel three, for example, Harlequin (in his traditional patched costume, also from the *commedia*) and Columbine are shown tête-à-tête in the background, while in the foreground the Clown taps his nose at the viewer to enjoin secrecy. The distribution of characters, the exaggerated postures, the elaborate costumes, the proscenium arch and curtains behind the figures exhibit the clearly theatrical visual paradigm. Lift the flap, and the scene changes: the Clown remains, but is now greeted not by the lovers, but by two washerwomen. The accompanying text describes the changed scene as follows:

62 (*top*) Sayer's *Harlequin Skeleton* (1772), with none of the flaps lifted. This example has been hand-coloured and so would have sold at the higher price listed on the cover: one shilling. The colouring matches that in another Bodleian copy, Dep. e.516.
(*bottom*) When the top flap in panel three of *Harlequin Skeleton* is lifted, Harlequin and Columbine disappear and are replaced by two washerwomen.

Oxford, Bodleian Library, Opie E 12.

Here Harlequin with Columbine
Is telling of his whole design
The prying Clown has found them out
And mean to tell what they're about
But Harlequin has marked the fool
And will ere long his courage cool.

The Old Man from his Information
The Subject treats with Speculation
How Harlequin is sadly fretted
To be in such a manner treated
Determined to no longer be
The Subject of their raillery.

The Old anatomist is seen
Who has a Daughter fair I ween
Whose name is called Columbine
Beloved much by Harlequine
Who tries with all his changefull art
To win the gentle ladies heart.

The simple Clown is struck with fear
To see the Skeleton so near
But by and by you'll find it true
He will have something else to do
Proceed and then with all my heart
I'll tell you more in second part.

Alas poor Clown in piteous taking
No doubt his silly heart is aking
That doth not know whether absconding
But widely think it death adauncing
Matt manfully he cries out yander
But turn it down and you'll see further.

Fair Columbine is now in view
Constant to Harlequin and true
Let his disguise be what it will
She knows him for her lover still
If you go on upon my word
You will see more in part the third.

My Harlequin with magic Sword
Has with the Clown kept to his word
That Harley may both wash & scrub
Perfue the Subject to the end
You'll find the meaning then my friend.

The Old Man here is in surprise
And views the scene with staring eyes
He vengeance vows but how and when
He thinks it right to think again
But what he will do time must shew
If you proceed perhaps you'll know.

Here Harley shews his proper shape
And will no longer be an ape
The Old Man stares to see him there
And well he may no doubt would swear
But turn it down and then my friend
Give your opinion from the end.

Old daddy Groot at last complies
And views them with indulgent eyes
He gives his blessing to the pair
And each is happy ev'ry where
The author will be happy too
If all to buy the book perfue.

Sly Harlequin with magic Sword
Has with the Clown kept to his word
The ladies [*sic*] hoop is made a Tub
That Harley may both wash & scrub

In the theatre, Harlequin's high jinks might have been achieved using trapdoors or other clever stagecraft: George Speaight notes that the bat 'could be used to change bits of scenery into something else, often with punning associations, as when a chimney pot was transformed into a chimney sweep or a bottle of blacking into a black woman'.[8] But here the magic produced by Harlequin's sword relies on the harlequinade's physical form as a book: the lifting of the flap is what reveals, indeed effects, the transformation of Columbine's hoop skirts into the bottom of the washerwoman's barrel, and the alert viewer appreciates the visual echo between crinoline and tub. The number of flaps limits the number of magical transformations, as another alternative name for the harlequinade turn-up – a metamorphosis – makes the story's magic part of the book's format.

Magic tricks

In the second half of the nineteenth century, the London firm Dean and Son (formerly Dean and Munday) published an extensive popular catalogue of children's books.[9] The Opies note Dean as the self-proclaimed originator of the movable book, when defined as a book 'contain[ing] pictures in which the characters could be "made to move and act in accordance with the incidents described in each story"', connecting the claim to the company's title *The Moveable Mother Hubbard* (1857).[10] As is often noted, the very nomenclature of Dean's publications makes for diverting reading: Dean advertises, to take just a few examples, Flexible-Faced Storybooks, cut-to-shape books, New Scenic Books, a Coloured Picture Nursery Sunday Book, Surprise Model Picture Books (a particularly unusual type of pop-up), Word Changing Chromo Toy Books and Cardboard Panorama Toy Books.

One of Dean's Victorian-era movables, *Transforming Performers* (not before 1873), continues the harlequinade's use of flaps to represent magical transformations.[11] The first verse in this volume, titled 'The Magician', counsels:

> If you turn up the folds of this magical book,
> And at its strange picture attentively look,
> You will conjure odd scenes which you ne'er saw before
> And which at each turn will amuse more and more.

The correspondence between magical book and movable book continues. However, the sort of magic represented, and the entertainment in which that magic originates, has changed. The image which accompanies this verse presents two different magicians, and a variety of magic tricks, through a diamond-shaped distribution of four flaps. Each folding back of an individual flap reveals a new section of the image, and an altered complete image. The first magician, with billowing sleeves, scarlet hose and admirable moustaches, seems a consummate professional; the text draws attention to his various accoutrements – a monkey, a white rabbit, magical glasses, golden hoops and so forth – which are also visible in the illustration (*figure* 63, *top*). He even has a signature exclamation: 'hey presto!' The second figure, revealed in full when all of the flaps are lifted (*figure* 63, *bottom*), seems a different sort of magician: this 'wizard with a long white beard, / A magic belt and pointed cap' is more mystical, his robes adorned with vaguely occult symbols. Nonetheless, he is engaged in the same sort of magic as the dashing first magician, with a similar set of magical objects and conjurer's bell.

It is notable that both of Dean's magicians evoke magic in terms of stage tricks rather than genuine sorcery. They practise what Simon During calls secular magic, magic that 'stakes no serious claim to contact with the supernatural' and is best represented by 'the technically produced magic of conjuring shows and special effects'.[12] There is a contrast, then, between magic in the harlequinade, which is real within the world of the narrative as it is real in the narratives to the original interludes (if also technically produced by a trick, by the book's flaps or the theatre's mechanics), and magic in *Transforming Performers*, which is acknowledged as a business, a staged repertoire. Here the magicians, with their rabbits and pigeons and hoop tricks, compete with the other transforming performers in the book, including acrobats, jugglers and trained animals, and with other popular entertainments: the circus and the menagerie. While the harlequinade represents the magic of a contemporary eighteenth-century theatrical spectacle, *Transforming Performers* takes its cue from Victorian cultures of enchantment as entertainment.

63 (*top*) The first magician from *Transforming Performers* (not before 1873) removes his magical bell from a white rabbit with a flourish. The movable mechanism works so that a whole image is presented to the viewer as each flap is lifted. (*bottom*) The second magician, as revealed when all four of the flaps in the diamond-shaped mechanism are lifted.

Oxford, Bodleian Library, Opie EE 287.

Lith. Emrik & Binger, Haarlem.

TRANSFORMING PERFORMERS:

WITH

SURPRISE PICTURES.

THE MAGICIAN.

If you turn up the folds of this magical book,
And at its strange pictures attentively look,
You will conjure odd scenes which you ne'er saw before,
And which at each turn will amuse more and more.

To begin with: a wizard, whom I once knew well,
He could make what he pleased fly out of a bell;
A monkey, a rabbit, a bird, or a lamp, —
Hey presto! he only his foot had to stamp!

Lith. Emrik & Binger, Haarlem.

Nursery rhymes

When movables retell nursery rhymes or fairy tales, they often choose formats that reflect something important about the original tale. Take the children's panorama book, made up of concertina-folded leaves that unfold to present a continuous image over a great length (often a number of feet). The surprisingly long extensions are always the major drawcard of the children's panorama in the Victorian era, just as size was the chief attraction of the original panoramas, the eighteenth- and nineteenth-century large-scale circular paintings invented by Robert Barker. (Barker was the first person to use the term 'panorama', in newspaper advertisements from 1791.) Once again, the focus on the physical size of the book can be seen, amusingly, in advertising material: Dean, for example, on the back cover of its shilling *Playtime Panorama* (c. 1880–1900), advertises more expensive series of panorama with the tagline *'Same style of book as this only longer'*. These series measured 8 feet 6 inches at a cost of 1s 6d, and 'about 10 feet' for 2s 6d.[13]

Bearing in mind the panorama's proudly declared grand scale, what would be an appropriate text to adapt? *The Flight of the Old Woman Who Was Tossed up in a Basket* (1844), 'Sketched & Etched by Aliquis' and published by D. Bogue of Fleet Street, pairs the expansive format of the panorama with a subject yet more grand: the sky.[14] Aliquis's panorama is an extension of the unglamorously magical nursery rhyme in which an old woman flies into the heavens 'to sweep the cobwebs from the sky'. The Opies

64 The text panel of Aliquis's *The Flight of the Old Woman Who Was Tossed up in a Basket* (1844), with the panorama folded to show panel six. Note that words and picture are separate: the only text on the individual panel is its number.

Oxford, Bodleian Library, Opie E 1.

he true and faithfull record of the flight of the
olde Woman who went up in a Baskett in the which
is shewne how she started on her Voyage, how she
advanced and how she finally arrived at the skye
together with many other thinges right pleasant
to beholde.

Here followeth the order of her Voyageas it is ex-
emplified in the several plates appertainyng here
unto together with a briefe explication, the which will
be found good and necessarie for y[e] righte under-
standyng thereof.

1. Here first is represented how certaine men
full mischieuouslie disposed, did, with much mirth
& great glee, tosse up y[e] olde woman in the baskett
by means of a blankett.

2 Here we see how the olde woman is inquired of by
one concerninge the place whereunto she wendeth her
waye.

3 How the olde woman was overtaken with much raine

4 The olde woman proceedeth on her voyage and look-
eth upward with great hope.

5 This man with lanthorne dogge & bushe of thorne pre-
'sentyng moonshine' as Maister Will Shakespeare saith
is here pourtrayed espying y[e] olde woman as she continueth to ascend

6 The olde woman still goeth upward and commenceth
her knitting caring not one figge for y[e] barkinge of the
dogge starre

7 The misfortune which befell y[e] olde woman in the
matter of her knitting

8 Here is y[e] great & dreadfull attack made upon y[e] olde
woman by divers birds and noisome beastes the
which she with great braverie and successe withstand-
eth.

9 The further progress of y[e] olde woman in y[e] which she
passeth many moones.

10 The olde woman here commenceth her worke in y[e]
skye the which she findeth full loathsome by reason
of the manie & great spyders which have for long time
bygone woven their webbes therein.

May her goode Work prosper.

include an image from Aliquis's *Flight* – from the very copy discussed here, in fact – alongside the entry for the rhyme in their *Oxford Dictionary of Nursery Rhymes*. The verse was popular in the Victorian era; it not only appeared in nursery collections, but Dickens also made 'the little old woman of the Child's … Rhyme' one of Esther Summerson's monikers in *Bleak House* (1852–53), quoting two lines.[15] The old woman's journey runs upwards along the panorama in a wordless, continuous series of numbered images, while the text is included in a separate key that identifies each panel by its number and explains or reflects on the action depicted (*figure 64*). (*Flight*'s twin panorama, the earlier *Pictorial Humpty Dumpty* from 1843, organises the book horizontally rather than vertically, with the panorama's length used to show a line of the King's men toppling backward, over and off the page.[16]) *Flight* plays with the scale of the sky and the scale of the book, including the panorama's length (7 feet) on the back cover and having its final image, an angled street sign, point downwards to earth and upwards 'Ad Infinitum': out of the book and into real space.

Individual images alter perspective, embedding visual tricks and jokes as another facet of scale: the old woman figures as large in some images, small in others, as her trip progresses. In panel five, for example, she appears only as a speck at the top of the image (*figure 65, bottom*). In the foreground is a much larger figure, a man in the moon equated in the text with the 'man, with lantern, dog, and bush of thorn' who '[p]resenteth Moonshine' from the play within a play in *A Midsummer Night's Dream*.[17] Like later self-conscious picture books from the twentieth and twenty-first centuries, this image centralises acts of looking, here by having the man in the moon gaze through a telescope at the old woman. The visual education that the illustration offers to the young reader is just as vital as the allusion to Shakespeare or the mock archaisms of the text, which signal its status as a re-imagining of folk material. By the next image, the composition has changed considerably (*figure* 65, *top*). The old woman is at the centre of the picture, her posture – head down, attention absorbed in her knitting – signalling her disregard for the 'dogge starre' at bottom right which barks at her from a celestial doghouse. Here it is the visual pun that piques the viewer's attention. The increased size of the panorama provides scope for envisioning the rhyme and its expanding fantasy world, scope in fact for considering the implications of the phrase *ad infinitum*.

Fairy tales

Most of the movable books discussed so far rely on simple paper engineering widely utilised in both book and non-book items before being redeployed in the juvenile market. By contrast, the books produced by Ernest Nister in the last decades of the nineteenth century are more complex: their movable-ness is historically and materially premised on 'the manufacture of tough papers and thin card' and 'the intrusion of modelling processes upon

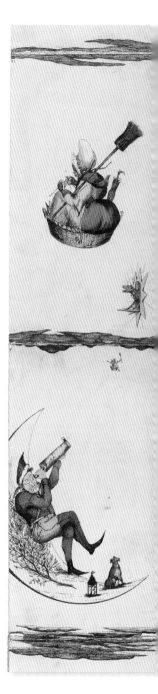

the conventional book-block', two key features of the movable identified by Brian Alderson.[18] Nister's colour printing operations, based in Nuremberg but with offices in London and distribution in the USA via Dutton, were so sophisticated that representatives from the British government visited them as part of a (somewhat anxious) review of German technical education in 1896. Nister was particularly famous for dissolving-picture books, in which one picture turns into another when a tab or ribbon is pulled. Nister used a variety of constructions; for example, vertical and horizontal dissolves, with pictures divided into slats and interlaid, and many different disc-shaped ones. These books are typically mini-anthologies of verse by such popular songwriters as Frederic Weatherly and Clifton Bingham. Black-and-white illustrations feature throughout the books, alongside dissolve pieces every few pages. The quality of Nister's chromolithography and its level of material innovation have garnered more approval than the some-times mawkish register of the texts or the aesthetic qualities of the illustrations. There is a sense that while Lothar Meggendorfer, Nister's fellow luminary from the so-called first Golden Age of movables in the late nineteenth and early twentieth centuries, produced movables that are urban, urbane and irreverent, Nister's are pastoral, silly and sentimental.

This may be true, but Nister's sentimental pastoralism lends itself to magical subject matter, particularly the fairy tale and (as I shall discuss in the next section) the fairy itself, in a way that Meggendorfer's register does not. One of the publisher's favourite

65 (*top*) The explanatory text for panel six of Aliquis's *Flight* reads, 'The olde woman still goeth upward and commenceth her knittinge caring not one figge for ye barking of the dogge starre'. The clouds at the edges of the panel mask the folds.
(*bottom*) The text for panel five reads, '"This man with lanthorne dogge & bushe of thorne presentyng moonshine" as Maister Will Shakespeare saith is here pourtrayed espyinge ye olde woman as she continueth to ascend.'

Oxford, Bodleian Library, Opie E 1.

ways to organise the paired images of the dissolving picture is by means of a fairy-tale connection. Sometimes this takes the form of a basic recognition of the similarity between two characters from different stories. In other examples, fairy-tale personages have read about other fairy-tale personages. There are fairy-tale exposés, where the text lets the reader in on an unknown link between two characters or a secret aspect of the tale (titles include 'How It Happened' and 'The Wonderland Mail').[19]

And, finally, there are continuations of tales and nursery rhymes. Take a poem called 'The End of the Story' in the Nister book *The Fairies Playtime* (not before 1899), a disc-dissolve book in which the circular pictures are segmented into a number of slats, the slats of the upper image overlaying the lower and moving beneath it when the ribbon is pulled. Written by Bingham, 'The End of the Story' has Cinderella and Old Mother Hubbard – strange bedfellows, to be sure – move in together.[20] Cinderella, after her wedding, 'recollected she'd once read / Poor Mother Hubbard's story'. This in itself is noteworthy: Cinderella is not usually a fairy-tale heroine who is well-read, in marked contrast to, say, Beauty. (Both Madame Le Prince de Beaumont's early version of the tale and Disney's 1991 *Beauty and the Beast* make that heroine a keen reader.) But the outlandish result of Cinders's reading is yet more remarkable:

> She made her come and live at Court,
> With servants five and twenty;
> So Mother Hubbard's happy now—
> Her dog gets bones in plenty!

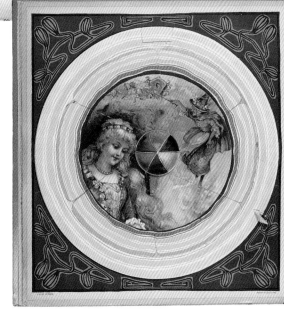

The End of the Story.

*N*O doubt you've read in Fairy Tale
Of poor Old Mother Hubbard,
Who could not find her dog a bone,
So empty was her cupboard!

Of Cinderella, too, you've heard,
By sisters so ill-treated;
I'll tell you now exactly how
Their stories were completed.

When Cinderella and her Prince
Were wedded all in glory,
She recollected she'd once read
Poor Mother Hubbard's story!

She made her come and
live at Court,
With servants five and twenty,
So Mother Hubbard's
happy now—
Her dog gets bones
in plenty!

66 (*top*) Dissolve image of Old Mother Hubbard from *The Fairies Playtime*. The book is a segmented disc dissolve. Note the beautiful *mise en page*, a Nister hallmark.
(*bottom*) Dissolve image of Cinderella. This image is also used in another Nister dissolving-picture book in the Opie Collection, *Little Folk's Peep Show* (189–). Repurposing images is common practice in Nister.

Oxford, Bodleian Library, Opie EE 28.

As is typical, the dissolving pictures offer episodes from the original tales rather than the text's fanciful blending of folklore. Old Mother Hubbard is shown with a dancing dog and cat, the image conflating the ninth and tenth stanzas of the rhyme: Mother Hubbard's dog feeding a cat, and dancing a jig (*figure 66, top*).[21] The dissolve picture of Cinderella shows the girl in her finery, surrounded by a smoky cloud that seems to be a kind of thought bubble; within the cloud the Fairy Godmother raises her wand and the pumpkin-coach awaits (*bottom*). The dissolve images depict the characters in a tone congruent with their respective tales: gauzy reverie for the glamorous magic of Cinderella, and sharp comical mayhem for the more com-

monplace magic of Old Mother Hubbard's domestic beast fable. Moreover, Nister makes the mechanics of the transformation beautiful in themselves: the rainbow edging around the Cinderella image creates a swirling, almost kaleidoscopic effect (*figure 67*).

Fairies and Fairyland

In many cases the magic spaces of Nister books are syncretic: characters from different nursery rhymes or fairy tales interact with one another in a single space. These worlds, variously called

67 The image of Old Mother Hubbard and Cinderella from *The Fairies Playtime* mid-dissolve. The rainbow patterning of the decorative border for the Cinderella image gives a kaleidoscopic effect when the ribbon tab is pulled.

Oxford, Bodleian Library, Opie EE 28.

Fairyland, Nursery Rhyme or Nursery-Tale Land, Wonderland and Storybook Land, reflect a knowing attitude to children's folk and fairy traditions. Tongue-in-cheek, rather than credulous, approaches to magic are encouraged. In other examples, though, the figuring of actual fairies and the space of Fairyland as a place where fairies dwell is more closely involved with the dynamic between belief and disbelief which so often informs children's literature.

Magical space is well represented by the pop-up mechanisms which have been archetypal of the movable form. Nister pop-up books usually include longer stories instead of the short verses common in the dissolving-picture books, and sometimes feature contributions from well-known children's authors. In E. Nesbit's story 'Naughty Noel' in *Peeps into Fairyland* (*c*. 1895), the eponymous protagonist refuses to 'believe in the fairies, and as people can believe in anything if they only try hard enough, of course this was quite his own fault. At any rate, so the fairies thought.'[22] The story involves Noel, accompanied by his sister Nina, visiting Fairyland and meeting fairies who mock his disbelief. (The children are in fact given a choice between Fairylands, and decide to go to the 'English Fairyland'.) Illustrated throughout in black and white, the story's one glorious full-colour pop-up image, which extends from the page in three dimensions when the book is opened (this common technique is called hinge projection), is captioned 'The Procession of Nursery Rhymes'. The pop-up shows such recognisable figures as Little Boy Blue, Little Red

Riding Hood, the Knave of Hearts, Puss in Boots and a fairy Mother Hubbard with a winged dog: a blend of fairy-tale and nursery-rhyme characters (*figure* 68). There is a definite moralism to what Ruskin called the child's 'inventive and believing power, – the *besoin de croire*' here.[23] Dick Whittington, for example, takes umbrage when Noel says 'I believe in *you*, old chap, because you're in history'; Dick's response is: 'Not a bit of it … don't you think it. I'm a fairy-tale person like the others.' The story rejects Noel's recourse to historical fact instead of fairy magic, and the child's readiness to believe is as much applauded by Nesbit as by J.M. Barrie in *Peter Pan* (1904) – its first performance roughly a decade after this book – wherein children clapping to demonstrate their belief in fairies is enough to ensure fairies' continued existence.

68 Noel and Nina visit 'the English Fairyland' in *Peeps into Fairyland* (c.1895). The top 'grotto' or scenic panel of the pop-up is the same as that in figure 69, but printed in a different colourway.

Oxford, Bodleian Library, Opie EE 219.

The pop-up can physically realise something of the wonder of the journey into Fairyland. M.A. Hoyer's unremarkable story in *Peeps into Fairyland* owes much to the general contours – if not the moral tone – of Hans Christian Andersen's fairy tale 'The Snow Queen' (1845), from the mock-Scandinavian names of the child protagonists Snaedrup and Fluflok to the Snow Queen herself, her attendant ice sprites so like the snow bees in Andersen's tale. However, the story is noteworthy for a lovely disposition of image and word, for using the movable piece to embody the children's fantastical journey. The text has the children travelling through a tunnel: 'It was very dark and cold, but there was a light far away at the end, and when they reached it, they stepped into a large place full of light and colour!' The pop-up image (*figure* 69), projecting

out in stark contrast to the flat facing page, spatialises the change from a dark tunnel to the 'light and colour' of the Snow Queen's enchanted palace. The pop-up image comprises two panels extending from a back page printed with wintry scenery, a benevolently smiling snowman and fairies looking on. The middle panel shows the two fur-clad children meeting the Snow Queen, who sits not on the throne we hear of in Hoyer's story, but on a giant snowball. While Hoyer's 'The Fairy Fir-Cones' is by no means a classic of children's literature, as Andersen's 'The Snow Queen' is, the pop-up strengthens the textual depiction of the snowy magical realm: the pop-up piece realises the story's magic in a way that is unavailable to the standard book.

The magic of finger and thumb

Nister's pop-up or dissolving-picture adaptations of fairy tale and nursery rhyme re-present extremely familiar stories and magical subjects in novel formats. Nister books are part of the late Victorian gift book market, as their attractive page layouts and Christmas themes show. The numerous presentation inscriptions in Nister titles from the Opie Collection reveal this process in action: 'For Georgina / with Uncle George's best love / Xmas 1896' in *The Robins at Home* (*c*.1895), 'Many Happy Returns of your Birthday / Love & best wishes to Lucy from Rose J. Bywater' in *Transformation Pictures and Comical Fixtures* (*c*.1896), 'To dear Harry with much love from his Cousin Grace' – Cousin Grace has drawn a star and clouds around her message – in *Something New for Little Folk* (191?).[24]

However, even movables that are not marketed as gift books involve the repackaging of magic. This is present in the frame for *Flight*, with a note on the cover which reads 'Nb. The purchasers of this work may rely upon receiving the earliest information of the return of the Old Woman', the magic of the story sold as a contemporary news item just like the type which could be read in Nister's 'Wonderland Mail'. Harlequinades might have acted as souvenirs of particular plays in the eighteenth century; as Jacqueline Reid-Walsh has shown, theatre-going in this period was a pastime that could involve children.[25] If harlequinades were souvenirs, the transformation of the experience of a play into the story and pictures of the harlequinade, which the child might take home and treasure, seems – as much as the tapping of Harlequin's bat – magical. Moreover, the contemporary fascination with computer-generated imagery and animation as it relates to fantasy might remind us of these movables: film franchises for children continue to make the form in which magical narratives come to the viewer a crucial feature of the enchantment.

Most importantly, in the movable it is the reader's participation that creates the book's magic. This is a feature of *Harlequin Skeleton*'s coaxing addresses to the reader, like 'turn it down, and you'll see further', which keep the story and its metamorphoses going. *The Bottle Conjurer* (1780), a William Tringham harlequinade, layers magical subject matter by having the titular conjurer produce none other than Harlequin himself, and by having the conjurer bestow Harlequin with his 'artful wand', which then becomes Harlequin's 'Magick Sword'.[26] But there are still further layers: for the magic belongs to the reader, too. In the second panel of *The Bottle Conjurer*, Harlequin's upper half emerges from the bottle, the rim of which corresponds to the join between flaps:

> Behold by his amazeing [*sic*] skill,
> He's rising gently to your will:
> In time he will his Tricks display,
> To make you Innocently gay.

While Harlequin rises from the bottle by the magician's 'amazeing' skill, he at the same time 'ris[es] gently to your will', the direct address securing a sense of reader participation in the trick. The same is true of the direct address at the beginning of *Transforming Performers*: reading the book correctly lets the reader 'conjure odd scenes which you ne'er saw before'. In Nister's *The Children's Wonderland* (*c.*1900), author Helen Marion Burnside uses the phrase 'the magic of finger and thumb'. The child's physical process of reading enchants the book, as the reader turns the pages to effect the magical transformations.

Conclusion

While I have focused on movables only up until the twentieth century, later inheritors of the tradition produce astounding movables that continue to use magic or magical subject matter.

...zerie

...long been said to roam
...to find them.

...THER, AND CLAW
...ween an eagle and a lion, the
...thousand years ago to the
...rently sculpted its image into
...emonic serpents and faith-
...ures. Like the unicorn, the
...often featured in the coats
...medieval Europe.

Two
talented
dancers
hidden beneath
an elaborate *Barong Ket*
costume can bring the
beast to life, dancing
and teasing bystanders
during local village
celebrations.

■ BATTLE
THE CE...
Fable and ... fierce rivalry
between ... rn and the
Lord ... or lion. Stories
of the ... popularized the
majest ... ast as a symbol
of E...

■ WINGS OF FLAME
The mighty phoenix of Western
...th is a huge pheasant-like bird with
...nson and gold plumage. After living for
...hundred years, this majestic solitary
...ature sets its cinnamon-twig nest afire
...nd bursts into flame, then rises from the
...ashes to live again.

■ BEASTLY PROTECTORS
Statues of *haetae*, a guardian
lion-dog sometimes depicted
with a unicorn horn, shield
the royal palace in Seoul, South
Korea, from natural disasters,
particularly from nearby
Mount Gwanaksan,
which was mistakenly
believed to be
a volcano.

■ THE GRIFFIN'S HOOFED COUSIN
Conjured in medieval legend, a hippogriff is the
offspring of a griffin and a horse, two mortal enemies.
The Renaissance poem *Orlando Furioso* describes
it as a fierce fairy mount, faster than lightning.

■ MILK FOR ALL
The freckled fairy cow,
...common to Celtic lore, was
...ed to give enough milk for
...village during times of
...ught and famine, but she would
...pear if treated cruelly.

...ough treacherous Arctic
waters—but only if treated to a sample of the first catch.

The famous pop-up artist Vojtech Kubasta produced a series of fairy-tale pop-ups for the Prague-based publishing company Artia from the 1950s onward, including movable adaptations of Cinderella, Little Red Riding Hood and Sleeping Beauty. How-to books in the pop-up medium, like Heinemann's *Pop-Up Book of Magic Tricks* (1983) or, fifteen years later, Orchard's *Best Pop-Up Magic Book Ever!* (1998), cannot help but recall *Transforming Performers*.[27] The fact that these books are not just movables about magic, but movables of magic in which the book encourages the reader's own magical performances, is a significant adaptation. To take just one example in detail, the foremost maker of pop-up books today, the American paper engineer Robert Sabuda, has released a number of fairy-tale pop-ups as well as other movable takes on magical subject matter. *Fairies and Magical Creatures* (2008), a mock encyclopaedia produced with Matthew Reinhart, has not one but multiple pop-up pieces on every double-page spread. One central pop-up piece figures 'the fairy realm' in terms of the space of the book and the movable's ability to augment that space in magical ways. Another has magical creatures drawn from a variety of mythological traditions erupting from the page courtesy of Sabuda's signature virtuoso paper engineering (*figure* 70).[28] The magical movable continues to find a readership in the twenty-first century.

70 (*previous page*) *Fairies and Magical Creatures* (2008), by Matthew Reinhart and Robert Sabuda, brings the magic movable into a new millennium.

Notes and references

Introduction

NOTES

1. C.S. Lewis, *Surprised by Joy*, Bles, London, 1955, p. 74.
2. J.R.R. Tolkien, 'On Fairy Stories', in *The Monsters and the Critics, and Other Essays*, HarperCollins, London, 2006, p. 153.

Chapter 1

NOTES

1. E. Eager, *Seven-Day Magic*, Harcourt, New York, 1999, pp. 1, 12.
2. C.S. Lewis, *The Voyage of the Dawn Treader*, Puffin, Harmondsworth, 1979, p. 129.
3. Ibid., p. 130.
4. Ibid., p. 132.
5. C.S. Lewis, *An Experiment in Criticism*, Cambridge, Cambridge University Press, 1992, p. 141.
6. S. Cooper, *The Dark Is Rising*, Puffin, Harmondsworth, 1992, pp. 115–16.
7. Ibid., p. 122.
8. U.K. Le Guin, *Steering the Craft*, The Eighth Mountain Press, Portland OR, 1998, p. 19.
9. U.K. Le Guin, *The Farthest Shore*, Puffin, Harmondsworth, 1975, pp. 171–2.
10. J.R.R. Tolkien, 'On Fairy-Stories', in *Tree and Leaf*, Allen & Unwin, London, 1975, p. 52.
11. See P. Dooley, 'Magic and Art in Ursula Le Guin's Earthsea Trilogy', *Children's Literature* 8, 1980, p. 109.
12. *Oxford English Dictionary*, s.v. *abracadabra*.
13. Diana Wynne Jones, *The Magicians of Caprona*, Arrow, London, 1987, p. 68.
14. Johann Wolfgang von Goethe, 'Der Zauberlehrling', in *Selected Verse*, Penguin, London, 1986, pp. 173–7.
15. U.K. Le Guin, *A Wizard of Earthsea*, Puffin, Harmondsworth, 1975, p. 34.
16. V. Walker, *The Winter of Enchantment*, Bobbs-Merrill, Indianapolis, 1969, p. 38.
17. D. Duane, *So You Want to Be a Wizard*, Harcourt, San Diego CA, 1996, pp. 6–7.
18. Ibid., p. 7.
19. G. Nix, *Lirael*, HarperCollins, London, 2001, p. 596.
20. T. Pratchett, *Hogfather*, Corgi, London, 2006, p. 271.
21. D. Steer, *Wizardology*, Templar, Dorking, 2005.
22. B. Sleigh, *Carbonel*, Puffin, London, 2005, pp. 161–2.
23. Ibid., p. 164.
24. E. Goudge, *Linnets and Valerians*, Puffin, London, 2001, p. 109.
25. Ibid., p. 118.
26. J.K. Rowling, *Harry Potter and the Philosopher's Stone*, Bloomsbury, London, 1997, pp. 52–3.
27. J. Stroud, *The Amulet of Samarkand*, Doubleday, London, 2003, pp. 68–9.
28. For instance, the charitable http://grinhamlatin.wetpaint.com/page/Latin+in+Harry+Potter?t=anon, which glosses over all Rowling's mistakes. See D. Purkiss, 'From Bedford Falls to Pottersville: Harry Potter, Consuming Narratives, and Bad Writing', *Journal of Children's Literature Studies*, vol. 5, no. 1, 2008.

29. J. Stephens, *The Emerald Atlas*, Doubleday, London, 2007, p. 91.

30. V. French, *The Snow Dragon*, Doubleday, London, 1999, n.p.

31. E. Nesbit, *The Book of Beasts*, in *The Last of the Dragons and Some Others*, Harmondsworth, Puffin, 1982, pp. 19–35, p. 25.

32. A. Garner, *The Moon of Gomrath*, HarperCollins, London, 2010, p. 217.

33. Ibid., p. 119.

34. See A.E. Waite, *The Book of Ceremonial Magic*, London, 1913, p. 259.

35. Garner, *The Moon of Gomrath*, p. 210.

36. For example, *commentur* is a third person plural verb, but there are no plural nouns in the sentence to act as a subject; 'there stands a superior map' and 'give the mountain and my enemies' are nonsense, and there are a few words which are either misspelled (perhaps missing contraction marks?) or simply made up (*bient, omviestra*).

37. Oxford, Bodleian Library, MS. Ashmole 1406, part I, fol. 53r.

38. J.C. Hirsh, 'Credulity and Belief: The Role of Postconditions in the Late Medieval Charm', *Preternature*, vol. I, no. 1, 2012, pp. 130–45; and see also J. Roper, *English Verbal Charms*, FF Communications, vol. 136, no. 288, Academia Scientarum Fennica, Helsinki, 2005.

FURTHER READING

Davies, O., *Grimoires: A History of Magic Books*, Oxford University Press, Oxford, 2009.

Garner, A., *The Voice That Thunders*, Harvill, London, 1997.

Hirsh, J.C., 'Credulity and Belief: The Role of Postconditions in the late Medieval Charm', *Preternature*, vol. I, no. 1, 2012, pp. 130–45.

James, E., and F. Mendlesohn (eds), *The Cambridge Companion to Fantasy Literature*, Cambridge University Press, Cambridge, 2012.

Le Guin, U.K., *Steering the Craft*, The Eighth Mountain Press, Portland OR, 1998.

Lerer, S., *Children's Literature: A Reader's History*, University of Chicago Press, Chicago, 2008.

Philip, N., *A Fine Anger*, Collins, London, 1981.

Rose, J., *The Case of Peter Pan*, Macmillan, London, 1984.

Tatar, M., *Enchanted Hunters: The Power of Stories in Childhood*, Norton, New York, 2009.

Todorov, T., *The Fantastic: A Structural Approach to a Literary Genre*, Cornell University Press, Ithaca NY, 1975.

Zipes, J., *Sticks and Stones*, Routledge, New York, 2000.

Chapter 2

NOTES

1. A. and E. Keary, *The Heroes of Asgard and the Giants of Jötunheim; or, The Week and its Story*, David Bogue, London, 1857, p. 5.

2. Ibid., pp. 6–7.

3. D. Wynne Jones, *Eight Days of Luke*, Collins, London, 2000, p. 114.

4. Ibid., p. 164.

5. W. Wägner, *Asgard and the Gods: The Tales and Traditions of Our Northern Ancestors, Forming a Complete Manual of Norse Mythology, Adapted from the Work of Dr W. Wägner by M.W. McDowall and ed. by W.S.W. Anson, with Numerous Illustrations*. Routledge, London, 1880, p. 128.

6. Ibid., p. 137.

7. Ibid., p. 26.

9. Ibid., p. 21.

10. A.S. Byatt, *Ragnarok*, Canongate, Edinburgh, 2011.

11. W. Morris, *The Story of Sigurd the Volsung and the Fall of the Niblungs*, Ellis & White, London, 1877.

12. F. McCarthy, *William Morris: A Life for Our Time*, Faber, London, 2003, pp. 372, 290.

13. A. Wawn, *The Vikings and the Victorians: Inventing the Old Norse in Nineteenth-Century Britain*, D.S. Brewer, Cambridge, 2000, pp. 271–6.

14. R. Wagner, *The Rhinegold and The Valkyrie; Siegfried and The Twilight of the Gods*, trans. M. Armour; illustrations by A. Rackham, Heinemann, London, 1910/11.

15. C.S. Lewis, *Surprised by Joy*, Bles, London, 1955, p. 74.

16. C.S. Lewis, *Collected Letters*, 3 vols, ed. W. Hooper, Harper, San Francisco, 2004–07, vol. I, pp. 323–4.

17. C.S. Lewis, *The Lion, the Witch and the Wardrobe*, Bles, London, 1950.

18. Lewis, *Collected Letters*, vol. II, p. 630.

19. H. Carpenter, *The Inklings: C.S. Lewis, J.R.R. Tolkien, Charles Williams and Their Friends*, HarperCollins, London, 2006, p. 56.

20. *Brothers and Friends: The Diaries of Major Warren Hamilton Lewis*, ed. C.S. Kilby and M.L. Mead, Harper & Row, San Francisco, 1982, pp. 145–6.

21. J.R.R. Tolkien, *The Children of Húrin*, HarperCollins, London, 2007.

22. J.R.R. Tolkien, *The Lord of the Rings*, Allen & Unwin, 1954.

23. J.R.R. Tolkien, *The Hobbit*, 3rd edn, HarperCollins, London, 1966, p. 73.

24. Tolkien, *The Hobbit*, pp. 204–5.

25. J. Carr, *The Wagner Clan*, Faber, London, 2007, pp. 183–5.

26. F. Spotts, *Bayreuth: A History of the Wagner Festival*, Yale University Press, New Haven CT, 1994, p. 165.

27. Ibid., p. 192.

28. B.L. Picard, Preface to *Tales of the Norse Gods and Heroes*, Oxford University Press, Oxford, 1953.

29. M. Meek, 'Green, Roger Gilbert Lancelyn (1918–1987)', *Oxford Dictionary of National Biography*, Oxford University Press; http://ezproxy.ouls.ox.ac.uk:2117/view/article/39541, accessed 23 July 2012.

30. R. Lancelyn Green, *Myths of the Norsemen*, Bodley Head, London, 1960; *The Saga of Asgard*, Penguin, Harmondsworth, 1960.

31. R. Lancelyn Green, *C.S. Lewis*, Bodley Head, London, 1969, p. 134.

32. K. Crossley-Holland, *The Norse Myths*, Andre Deutsch, London, 1980.

33. K. Crossley-Holland, *Bracelet of Bones*, Quercus, London, 2012, p. 85.

34. Keary and Keary, *Heroes of Asgard*, p. 145.

35. A. Garner, *The Weirdstone of Brisingamen*, Collins, London, 1960; *The Moon of Gomrath*, Collins, London, 1963.

36. A. Garner, *The Weirdstone of Brisingamen*, Harper Collins, London, 2010, pp. 143, 147.

37. Ibid., p. 283.

38. J. Harris, *Runemarks*, Doubleday, London, 2007; *Runelight*, Doubleday, London, 2011.

39. Harris, *Runemarks*, p. 326.

40. www.guardian.co.uk/books/2007/mar/24/featuresreviews.guardianreview28, accessed 1 October 2009; M. Burgess, *Bloodtide*, Andersen, London, 1999.

41. www.melvinburgess.net, accessed 21 May 2009.

42. Picard, *Tales of the Norse Gods and Heroes*, p. 6.

43. M. Burgess, *Bloodsong*, Andersen, London, 2005.

44. C.S. Lewis, 'The Dethronement of Power', in *Tolkien and the Critics*, ed. N.D. Isaacs and R.A. Zimbardo, Notre Dame University Press, South Bend IN, 1968, p. 15.

45. F. Simon, *The Sleeping Army*, Faber, London, 2012.

46. *Thor*, 2011, dir. Kenneth Branagh, starring Chris Hemsworth, Natalie Portman and Tom Hiddleston.

47. 'The Seeress's Prophecy' vv. 59–61, in *The Poetic Edda*, trans. C. Larrington, Oxford World's Classics, Oxford University Press, Oxford, 1996, p. 12.

FURTHER READING

Clark, D., 'Old Norse Made New: Past and Present in Modern Children's Literature', in D. Clark and C. Phelpstead (eds), *Old Norse Made New: Essays on the Post-Medieval Reception of Old Norse Literature and Culture*, Viking Society, London, 2007.

Clunies Ross, M., *The Norse Muse in Britain 1750–1820*, Parnaso, Trieste, 1998.

Evans, J., 'The Dragon-Lore of Middle Earth: Tolkien and Old English and Old Norse Tradition', in G. Clark and D. Timmons (eds), *J.R.R. Tolkien and His Literary Resonances: Views of Middle-Earth*, Greenwood Press, Greenwood CT, 2000.

Guardian, www.guardian.co.uk/books/2011/aug/05/as-byatt-ragnarok-myth?intcmp=ilcnettxt3487.

Guardian, www.guardian.co.uk/books/2011/sep/04/ragnarok-canongate-as-byatt-review?intcmp=ilcnettxt3487

Larrington, C., 'Melvin Burgess's *Bloodtide* and *Bloodsong*: Sigmundr, Sigurðr and Young Adult Literature', in K. Schulz (ed.), *Eddische Götter und Helden – Milieus und Medien ihrer Rezeption*, Carl Winter, Heidelberg, 2011.

O'Donoghue, H., *From Asgard to Valhalla: The Remarkable History of the Norse Myths*, I.B. Tauris, London, 2007.

Shippey, T.A., *The Road to Middle-Earth: How J.R.R. Tolkien Created a New Mythology*, rev. and expanded edn, Harper Collins, London, 2005.

Wawn, A., *The Vikings and the Victorians: Inventing the Old Norse in Nineteenth-Century Britain*, D.S. Brewer, Cambridge, 2000.

Chapter 3

NOTES

1. C.S. Lewis (ed.), *George MacDonald: An Anthology*, Fount Paperbacks, London, 1983, p. 33.

2. G. MacDonald, *The Princess and Curdie*, Penguin, Harmondsworth, 1966, pp. 134; 160.

3. Ibid., pp. 73, 182.

4. E. Nesbit, *Five Children and It*, Penguin, Harmondsworth, 1959, p. 116.

5. Ibid., p. 116.

6. Ibid., p. 117.

7. C.S. Lewis, *The Magician's Nephew*, Collins Lions, London, 1980, p. 9.

8. R. Kipling, *Puck of Pook's Hill*, Puffin, Harmondsworth, 1987, p. 22.

9. Ibid., pp. 32, 83.

10. Ibid., p. 55.

11. Ibid., p. 203.

12. Ibid., p. 215.

13. M. Ward, *Planet Narnia: The Seven Heavens in the Imagination of C.S. Lewis*, Oxford University Press, Oxford, 2008, p. 237.

14. K. Kerby-Fulton, '"Standing on C.S. Lewis's Shoulders":

C.S. Lewis as Critic of Medieval Literature', *Medievalism: Inklings and Others*, ed. J. Chance, special issue of *Studies in Medievalism*, vol. 3, no. 3, 1991, pp. 257–78; 258.

15. C.S. Lewis, *The Discarded Image: An Introduction to Medieval and Renaissance Literature*, Cambridge University Press, Cambridge, 1994 (1964), p. 216.

16. A twelfth-century manuscript containing a Latin text of the *Marvels of the East* is held in the Bodleian: MS. Bodl. 614, http://treasures.bodleian.ox.ac.uk/The-Marvels-of-the-East.

17. M.Y. Miller, '"Of sum mayn meruayle, þat he myȝt trawe": *The Lord of the Rings* and *Sir Gawain and the Green Knight*', in *Medievalism: Inklings and Others*, pp. 45–66; 348.

18. J. Chance and D. Day, 'Medievalism in Tolkien: Two Decades of Criticism in Review', in *Medievalism: Inklings and Others*, pp. 375–87; 387.

19. S. Cooper, *The Dark Is Rising*, Puffin, London, 1976, p. 212.

20. M.D.C. Drout, 'Reading the Signs of Light: Anglo Saxonism, Education, and Obedience in Susan Cooper's *The Dark Is Rising*', *The Lion and the Unicorn*, vol. 21, no. 2, 1997, pp. 230–50.

21. S. Cooper, quoted in B. Harrison and G. Maguire (eds), *Innocence and Experience: Essays and Conversations on Childrens Literature*, Lothrop, Lee, and Shepard, Boston MA, 1987, p. 202.

22. A. Garner, *Elidor*, Collins Lions, London, 1974, p. 86.

23. A. Garner, *Boneland*, HarperCollins, London, 2012.

24. C. Fisher, *The Snow-Walker Trilogy*, Red Fox, London, 2003, p. 137.

25. Ibid., p. 138.

26. C. Butler, *Four British Fantasists: Place and Culture in the Children's Fantasies of Penelope Lively, Alan Garner, Diana Wynne Jones, and Susan Cooper*, Children's Literature Association and the Scarecrow Press, Lanham MD, 2006, p. x.

27. A.J. Lake, *The Coming of Dragons*, Bloomsbury, London, 2006, pp. 40, 64.

FURTHER READING

Butler, C., *Four British Fantasists: Place and Culture in the Children's Fantasies of Penelope Lively, Alan Garner, Diana Wynne Jones, and Susan Cooper*, Children's Literature Association and the Scarecrow Press, Lanham MD, 2006.

Cecire, M.S., 'Medievalism, Popular Culture and National Identity in Children's Fantasy Literature', *Studies in Ethnicity and Nationalism*, vol. 9, no. 3, 2009, pp. 395–409.

Cecire, M.S., '*Ban Welondes*: Wayland Smith in Popular Culture', in D. Clark and N. Perkins (eds), *Anglo-Saxon Culture and the Modern Imagination*, D.S. Brewer, Woodbridge, 2010, pp. 201–17.

James, E., and F. Mendlesohn (eds), *The Cambridge Companion to Fantasy Literature*, Cambridge University Press, Cambridge, 2012.

Lenz, M., and C. Scott (eds), *His Dark Materials Illuminated: Critical Essays on Philip Pullman's Trilogy*, Wayne State University Press, Detroit MI, 2005.

Manlove, C., *From Alice to Harry Potter: Children's Fantasy in England*, Cybereditions Corporation, Christchurch, New Zealand, 2003.

Mendlesohn, F., *Diana Wynne Jones: Children's Literature and the Fantastic Tradition*, Routledge, New York, 2005.

Oziewicz, M., *The Mythopoeic Fantasy Series of Ursula K. Le Guin, Lloyd Alexander, Madeleine L'Engle and Orson Scott Card*, McFarland, Jefferson NC, 2008.

Oziewicz, M., 'Christian, Norse and Celtic: Metaphysical Belief Structures in Nancy Farmer's *The Saxon Saga*', *Mythlore* 20, 2011, pp. 107–21.

Philip, N., *A Fine Anger: A Critical Introduction to the Work of Alan Garner*, Peter Lang, HarperCollins, London, 1981.

Rosenberg, T., et al. (eds), *Diana Wynne Jones: An Exciting and Exacting Wisdom*, Peter Lang, New York, 2002.

Shippey, T.A., *The Road to Middle-Earth: How J.R.R. Tolkien Created a New Mythology*, HarperCollins, London, 2005 (1983).

Chapter 4

NOTES

1. R. Baden-Powell, *Yarns for Boy Scouts*, Arthur Pearson, London, 1909, p. 142.

2. M. Rosenthal, 'Knights and Retainers: The Earliest Version of Baden-Powell's Boy Scout Scheme?', *Journal of Contemporary History* 15, 1980, pp. 603–17; 609.

3. Baden-Powell, *Yarns for Boy Scouts*, p. 117.

4. R. Baden-Powell, *Scouting for Boys: A Handbook for Instruction in Good Citizenship*, ed. E. Boehmer, Oxford University Press, Oxford, 2004, p. 214.

5. Ibid., p. 215.

6. J.T. Koch (ed.), *The Gododdin of Aneirin: Text and Context from Dark-Age North Britain*, University of Wales Press, Cardiff, 1997.

7. M.A. Faletra (ed.), *The History of the Kings of Britain*, Broadview, Peterborough, Ontario, 2008.

8. J. Weiss (ed.), *The Life of King Arthur*, Everyman, London, 1997.

9. A. Lynch, 'Le Morte Darthur for Children: Malory's

Third Tradition', in B.T. Lupack (ed.), *Adapting the Arthurian Legends for Children: Essays on Arthurian Juvenilia*, Palgrave Macmillan, Basingstoke and New York, 2004, p. 4.

10. For a facsimile edition, see R. Ascham, *The Scholemaster*, De Capo Press, Amsterdam, 1968. For a modern translation, see L.V. Ryan (ed.), *Roger Ascham, The Schoolmaster*, Cornell University Press, Ithaca NY, 1967.

11. Ascham, *The Scholemaster*, p. 27a.

12. Ibid., p. 27b.

13. Ibid., p. 27a.

14. J. Milton, 'Manso', in *The Riverside Milton*, ed. R. Flannagan, Houghton Mifflin, Boston MA, 1998, p. 234.

15. N. Crouch, *The History of the Nine Worthies of the World*, London, 1687, p. 127.

16. M. Girouard, *The Return to Camelot: Chivalry and the English Gentleman*, Yale University Press, New Haven CT and London, 1981, p. 178.

17. M. Grenby, 'Bibliography: The Resources of Children's Literature', in P. Hunt (ed.), *Understanding Children's Literature*, 2nd edn, Routledge, London, 1999, p. 148.

18. R. Southey (ed.), *The Byrth, Lyf and Actes of King Arthur; of his Noble Knyghtes of the Rounde Table, Theyr Mervellous Enquestes and Aduentures, Thachyeuing of the Sant Greal; and in the End Le Morte Darthur, with the Dolourous Deth and Departyng out of Thys Worlde of Them Al*, Longman, Hurste, Rees, Orme & Brown, London, 1817, p. xxvii.

19. Ibid., p. xxvii.

20. A. Tennyson, 'Gareth and Lynette', in *The Poems of Tennyson*, vol. 3, 2nd edn, ed. C. Ricks, Longman, Harlow, 1987, p. 255.

21. C. Ricks, 'Tennyson, Alfred, first Baron Tennyson (1809–1892)', *Oxford Dictionary of National Biography*, Oxford University Press, 2004; online edn, May 2006, www.oxforddnb.com/view/article/27137 (accessed 14 April 2012).

22. A. Tennyson, *Poems*, Edward Moxon, London, 1857.

23. T. Malory, *Le Mort Darthur*, illus. Aubrey Beardsley, J.M. Dent, London, 1893–94.

24. *The Poems of Tennyson*, vol. 3, ed. Ricks, p. 259.

25. E. Bulwer-Lytton, *King Arthur*, Henry Colburn, London, 1849, vol. I, p.32.

26. Ibid., vol. II, p. 137.

27. Ibid., vol. I, p. 32.

28. I. Bryden, 'Reinventing Origins: The Victorian Arthur and Racial Myth', in Shearer West (ed.), *The Victorians and Race*, Scolar, Aldershot, 1996, p. 144.

29. Tennyson, 'Gareth and Lynette', p. 285.

30. Lynch, 'Le Morte Darthur', p. 12.

31. J.T. Knowles, *The Story of King Arthur and His Knights of the Round Table*, Griffith & Farran, London, 1862, p. ii.

32. Ibid., p. ii.

33. Ibid., p. iii.

34. S. Lanier, *The Boy's King Arthur, being Sir Thomas Malory's History of King Arthur and His Knights of the Round Table*, Sampson Low, Marston, Searle & Rivington, London, 1880, p. xxii.

35. S. Lanier, *The Boy's King Arthur*, Dover, Mineola NY, 2006.

36. Girouard, *The Return to Camelot*, p. 168.

37. W. Morris, *The Defence of Guinevere, and Other Poems*, Bell & Daldy, London, 1858; W. Morris, *The Well at the World's End*, Longman, London, 1896.

38. C.S. Lewis, *Surprised By Joy: The Shape of my Early Life*, HarperCollins, London, 2002, p. 207.

39. C.S. Lewis, *The Magician's Nephew*, in *The Complete Chronicles of Narnia*, Collins, London, 2000, p. 18.

40. Lynch, 'Le Morte Darthur', p. 10.

41. C. Yonge, *The History of the Life and Death of the Good Knight Sir Thomas Thumb*, Hamilton Adams, London, 1855, p. 87.

42. Tennyson, 'Geraint and Enid', in *The Poems of Tennyson*, vol. 3, ed. Ricks, p. 375; Tennyson, 'Guinevere', in ibid., p. 538.

43. J.N. Couch, 'Howard Pyle's "The Story of King Arthur and His Knights" and the Bourgeois Boy Reader', *Arthuriana*, vol. XIII, no. 2, 2003, pp. 38–53; 46.

44. S. Brown, P. Clements and I. Grundy, 'Roma White', in *Orlando: Women's Writing in the British Isles from the Beginnings to the Present*, online database, Cambridge University Press, orlando.cambridge.org/protected/svPeople?people_tab=2&formname=r&heading=h&person_id=whit0#LateNovelsasBlancheWinder (accessed 12 April 2012).

45. B. Winder (Roma White), *King Arthur and His Knights*, Ward, Lock, London, 1937, p. 15.

46. Ibid., pp. 50, 178.

47. A. and L. Lang, *The Book of Romance*, Longmans, Green, London, 1902, p. 132.

48. Lynch, 'Le Morte Darthur', p. 17.

49. H. Pyle, *Sir Lancelot and His Companions*, Chapman & Hall, London, 1907, p. 340.

50. W.B. Forbush, *The Boy Problem*, Westminster Press, Philadelphia PA, 1902, p. 140.

51. K.J. Harty, '"The Knights of the Square Table": The Boy Scouts and Thomas Edison make an Arthurian Film', *Arthuriana*, vol. IV, no. 4, 1994, pp. 313–23; 322.

52. W.B Forbush and D. Forbush, *The Knights of King*

Arthur: How to Begin and What to Do, 1915, archived online by the Camelot Project at the University of Rochester, www.lib.rochester.edu/camelot/KOKA.htm (accessed 13 April 2012).

53. Bodleian Library, Oxford, Per.9419 d.34.
54. I am indebted to Helen Nightingale for bringing the continuing existence of the Knights of the Round Table to my attention.
55. Girouard, *The Return to Camelot*, p. 281.
56. Lanier, *The Boy's King Arthur*, illus. N.C. Wyeth, Charles Scribner, New York, 1917; Sidney Lanier, *The Boy's King Arthur: Being Sir Thomas Malory's History of King Arthur and His Knights of the Round Table*, Charles Scribner, New York, 1920.
57. R. Baden-Powell, *Young Knights of the Empire: Their Code and Further Scout Yarns*, J.B. Lippincott, London, 1917.
58. Girouard, *The Return to Camelot*, pp. 277–81.
59. Ibid., p. 169.
60. T.H. White, *The Once and Future King*, Voyager, London, 1996, p. 71.
61. C.S. Lewis, *That Hideous Strength: A Modern Fairy-Tale for Grown-Ups*, Bodley Head, London, 1945.
62. E. Vinaver, *The Works of Sir Thomas Malory*, rev. P.J.C. Field, Clarendon Press: Oxford, 1990.
63. R.L. Green, *King Arthur and His Knights of the Round Table*, Faber & Faber, London, 1953, pp. 94, 11.
64. Ibid., p. 17.
65. S. Cooper, *The Dark is Rising*, Puffin, London, 1996.
66. R.H. Thompson, 'Interview with Susan Cooper', in B.T. Lupack, ed., *Adapting the Arthurian Legends for Children: Essays on Arthurian Juvenilia*, Palgrave Macmillan, Basingstoke and New York, 2004, p. 164.
67. J. Steinbeck, *The Acts of King Arthur and His Noble Knights from the Winchester MSS. Of Thomas Malory and Other Sources*, ed. C. Horton, Farrar, Straus & Giroux, New York, 1976, p. 296.
68. Ibid., preliminary pages.
69. A. Garner, *The Weirdstone of Brisingamen: A Tale of Alderly*, Collins, London, 1960; *The Moon of Gomrath*, Collins, London, 1963.
70. A. Garner, *The Weirdstone of Brisingamen: 50th Anniversary Edition*, London, HarperCollins, 2010. 13.
71. C.S. Lewis, *The Voyage of the Dawn Treader*, in *The Complete Chronicles of Narnia*, Collins, London, 2000, p. 296.
72. C. Lindahl, 'Three Ways of Coming Back: Folkloric Perspectives on Arthur's Return', in Debra Mancoff (ed.), *King Arthur's Modern Return*, Routledge, London, 1998, pp. 13–30, 16–17.

73. R. Sutcliff, *The King Arthur Trilogy*, Red Fox, London, 1999; N. Philip, *The Tale of Sir Gawain*, Lutterworth, Cambridge, 1987; K. Crossley-Holland, *The Seeing Stone*, Collins, London, 2000; K. Crossley-Holland, *At the Crossing-Places*, Orion, London, 2001; K. Crossley-Holland, *King of the Middle March*, Orion, London, 2003; K. Crossley-Holland, *Gatty's Tale*, Orion, London, 2006.
74. M.A. Torregrossa, 'Once and Future Kings: The Return of King Arthur in the Comics', in Lupack (ed.), *Adapting the Arthurian Legends for Children* p. 253.
75. Ibid.
76. See B. Kane, *The Definitive Prince Valiant Companion*, Fantagraphics, Seattle WA, 2009; *Prince Valiant*, dir. H. Hathaway, Twentieth Century Fox, 1954; *Prince Valiant*, dir. A. Hockix, Constantin Film Produktion, 1997; D. Corbett, *The Legend of Prince Valiant*, The Family Channel, first aired 3 September 1991.
77. C. Claremont and H. Trimpe, *Captain Britain Weekly #1*, Marvel Comics UK, 13 October 1976.
78. M.W. Barr, B. Bolland, T. Austin, B. Patterson, D. Giordano, T. Wood and J. Costanza, *Camelot 3000: The Deluxe Edition*, DC Comics, New York, 2008.
79. M.Z. Bradley, *The Mists of Avalon*, Michael Joseph, London, 1983.
80. T. Pierce, *Alanna: The First Adventure*, Atheneum, New York, 1983; *In The Hand of the Goddess*, Atheneum, New York, 1984; *The Woman Who Rides Like a Man*, Atheneum, New York, 1986; *Lioness Rampant*, Atheneum, New York, 1988.
81. 'Interview with Tamora Pierce', 11 January 2011, Bookyurt. com, http://bookyurt.com/scouting/interviews/tamora-pierce-on-influences-fight-scenes-and-more/ (accessed 3 June 2012); for a discussion of Pyle's promotion of individualism see Couch, 'Howard Pyle's "The Story of King Arthur and His Knights" and the Bourgeois Boy Reader', pp. 40–42.
82. M. Stewart, *The Wicked Day*, Hodder & Stoughton, London, 1983; N. Springer, *I am Mordred*, Hodder Children's Books, London, 1998; M. Cabot, *Avalon High*, Macmillan Children's Books, London, 2006.
83. Springer, *I am Mordred*, p. 194.
84. P. Dickinson, *Merlin Dreams*, Victor Gollancz, London, 1988; P. Reeve, *Here Lies Arthur*, Scholastic, London, 2007.
85. *Merlin*, written by J. Jones, J. Michie, J. Capps and J. Murphy, Shine Television, 2008–12. First episode aired 20 September 2008.

FURTHER READING

Archibald, E., and A. Putter (ed.), *The Cambridge Companion to the Arthurian Legend*, Cambridge University Press, Cambridge, 2009.

Baden-Powell, R., *Scouting for Boys: A Handbook for Instruction in Good Citizenship*, ed. E. Boehmer, Oxford University Press, Oxford, 2004.

Fulton, H. (ed.), *A Companion to Arthurian Literature*, Blackwell, Oxford and Malden MA, 2009.

Harty, K.J. (ed.), *King Arthur on Film: New Essays on Arthurian Cinema*, McFarland, Jefferson NC, 1999.

Howey, A.F., and S.R. Reimer, *A Bibliography of Modern Arthuriana (1500–2000)*, D.S. Brewer, Cambridge, 2006.

Lupack, A. (ed.), *Arthurian Studies 51: New Directions in Arthurian Studies*, D.S. Brewer, Cambridge, 2002.

Lupack, A., 'Visions of Courageous Achievement: Arthurian Youth Groups in America', in K. Verduin (ed.), *Studies in Medievalism 6: Medievalism in North America*, D.S. Brewer, Cambridge, 2004.

Lupack, A., and B.T. Lupack, *King Arthur in America*, D.S. Brewer, Cambridge, 1999.

Lupack, A., and B.T. Lupack, *Illustrating Camelot*, D.S. Brewer, Cambridge, 2008.

Pearsall, D., *Arthurian Romance: A Short Introduction*, Blackwell, Oxford and Malden MA, 2003.

Rosenthal, M., *The Character Factory: Baden-Powell and the Origins of the Boy Scout Movement*, Collins, London, 1986.

Sklar, E., and D.L. Hoffman (ed.), *King Arthur in Popular Culture*, McFarland & Company, Jefferson NC, 2002.

Chapter 5

NOTES

1. For a discussion of the distinction between novelty books and movables, see Children's Books History Society, 'Novelty Books and Movables: Questions of Terminology', *Children's Books History Society Newsletter* 61, July 1998, p. 15. Throughout, I draw my terms from this useful, brief taxonomy.

2. On the *Astronomicum Caesareum*, see A. Grafton, 'Some Uses of Eclipses in Early Modern Chronology', *History of the Journal of Ideas* 64, 2003, p. 222; on the *Epitome*, see plate 38 in K.B. Roberts and J.D.W. Tomlinson, *The Fabric of the Body: European Traditions of Anatomical Illustration*, Clarendon Press, Oxford, 1992, pp. 168–9; on Llull, see J. Helfand, *Reinventing the Wheel*, Princeton Architectural Press, New York, 2002, p. 19.

3. B. Alderson, 'Bibliography and Children's Books: The Present Position', *The Library*, ser. 5, 32, 1977, p. 206.

4. For a manuscript turn-up from 1650, see entry number 33 in B. Alderson and F. de Marez Oyens, *Be Merry and Wise: Origins of Children's Book Publishing in England, 1650–1850*, Pierpont Morgan Library/Bibliographical Society of America/British Library/Oak Knoll Press, New York/London/New Castle DE, 2006, p. 22.

5. The uncut sheets, originally published by Benjamin Tabart, were acquired by William Darton Jr, and bound together with other materials by him. The shelfmark is Vet. A6 c.118. See J. Shefrin, *The Dartons: Publishers of Educational Aids, Pastimes and Juvenile Ephemera, 1787–1876*, Cotsen Occasional Press, Los Angeles, 2009, pp. 97–9.

6. C. Dickens, 'A Christmas Tree', *Household Words*, 21 December 1850, pp. 289–95; R.L. Stevenson, 'A Penny Plain and Twopence Coloured' (1884), in *Memories and Portraits*, Charles Scribner and Sons, New York, 1895, pp. 213–27.

7. *Harlequin's Invasion*, Robert Sayer, London, 1812 (1770), shelfmark Vet. A6 e.2603; *Harlequin Cherokee or the Indian Chiefs in London*, Robert Sayer, London, 1772, shelfmark Dep. e.508; *Harlequin Skeleton*, Robert Sayer, London, 1772, shelfmark Opie E 12; *Robinson Crusoe or Harlequin Friday, Part II*, E. Tringham, London, 1781, shelfmark Opie E 71. Although *Harlequin's Invasion* was first published in 1770, and in the Bodleian copy the original date of publication has not been changed, it is in fact a reissue watermarked 1812. No movables referred to in this chapter are paginated.

8. G. Speaight with B. Alderson, 'From Chapbooks to Pantomime', in J. Briggs, D. Butts and M.O. Grenby (eds), *Popular Children's Literature in Britain*, Ashgate, Aldershot, 2008, p. 89.

9. P.A.H. Brown, *London Publishers and Printers c.1800–1870*, British Library, London, 1982, p. 55.

10. I. and P. Opie, 'Books that Come to Life', *The Saturday Book* 34, 1975, p. 63.

11. *Transforming Performers: With Surprise Pictures*, Dean and Son, London, [not before 1873], shelfmark Opie EE 287. Date of publication suggested by Bodleian.

12. S. During, *Modern Enchantments: The Cultural Power of Secular Magic*, Harvard University Press, Cambridge MA, 2002, p. 1.

13. *Playtime Panorama*, Dean and Son, London, [c.1880–1900], shelfmark Johnson d.2133.

14. Aliquis, *The Flight of the Old Woman Who Was Tossed up in a Basket*, D. Bogue, London, [1844], shelfmark Opie E 1. Date of publication suggested by Bodleian.

15. I. and P. Opie (eds), *The Oxford Dictionary of Nursery Rhymes*, 2nd edn, Oxford University Press, Oxford, 1997,

pp. 521–3; C. Dickens, *Bleak House*, ed. S. Gill, Oxford University Press, Oxford, 1998, p. 97.

16. [Aliquis], *The Pictorial Humpty Dumpty*, [Tilt and Bogue], [London], 1843, shelfmark Opie E 38a. Author and imprint suggested by Bodleian.

17. *A Midsummer Night's Dream*, ed. P. Holland, Oxford University Press, Oxford, 1994, p. 239, 5.1.134–135. References are to act, scene, line.

18. B. Alderson, 'The Making of Children's Books', in M.O. Grenby and A. Immel (eds), *The Cambridge Companion to Children's Literature*, Cambridge University Press, Cambridge, 2009, p. 42.

19. *Transformation Pictures and Comical Fixtures*, Ernest Nister/E.P. Dutton, London/New York, [*c*.1896], shelfmark Opie EE 32; H.M. Burnside, *The Children's Wonderland*, illus. F. Hardy, Ernest Nister/E.P. Dutton, London/New York, [*c*.1900], shelfmark Opie EE 42. Dates of publication suggested by Bodleian.

20. C. Bingham, *The Fairies Playtime*, E.P. Dutton/Ernest Nister, New York/London, [not before 1899], shelfmark Opie EE 28. Date of publication suggested by Bodleian.

21. For a standard text and a discussion of the rhyme, see Opie and Opie, *Dictionary of Nursery Rhymes*, pp. 374–8.

22. F.E. Weatherly, *Peeps into Fairyland*, Ernest Nister/E. P. Dutton, London/New York, [*c*.1895], shelfmark Opie EE 219. Date of publication suggested by Bodleian. Weatherly acts as a sort of editor for this volume: some of the texts are attributed to him, some are unattributed and some (including the stories I discuss) are attributed to other authors.

23. J. Ruskin, 'Fairy Land: Mrs. Allingham and Kate Greenaway', in *The Complete Works of John Ruskin*, vol. XXXIII, ed. E.T. Cook and A. Wedderburn, George Allen/Longmans Green, London/New York, 1908, p. 329.

24. F.E. Weatherly, *The Robins at Home*, Ernest Nister/E.P. Dutton, London/New York, [*c*.1895], shelfmark Opie EE 244; C. Bingham, *Something New for Little Folk*, [Ernest Nister/E. P. Dutton], [London], [191?], shelfmark Opie

EE 31. Date of publication for *Robins at Home* suggested by Bodleian; imprint and date of publication for *Something New* suggested by National Union Catalog (NUC) of pre-1956 imprints.

25. J. Reid-Walsh, 'Pantomime, Harlequinades and Children in Late Eighteenth-Century Britain: Playing in the Text', *British Journal for Eighteenth-Century Studies* 29, 2006, pp. 413–25.

26. *The Bottle Conjurer*, William Tringham, London, 1780, shelfmark Opie E 30.

27. R. van der Meer, *The Pop-up Book of Magic Tricks: Flabbergast Your Friends with These Amazing Pop-Up Tricks!*, Heinemann, London, 1983; N. Sharratt, M. Johnstone and R. Fergusson, *The Best Pop-Up Magic Book Ever!*, Orchard, London, 1998.

28. M. Reinhart and R. Sabuda, *Fairies and Magical Creatures*, Walker Books, London, 2008.

FURTHER READING

Chester, T., *Movable Books in the Renier Collection*, Occasional List no. 3, Bethnal Green Museum of Childhood, London, 1988.

Fox, G., 'Movable Books', in K. Reynolds and N. Tucker (eds), *Children's Book Publishing in Britain since 1945*, Scolar Press, Aldershot, 1998, pp. 86–109.

Haining, P., *Movable Books: An Illustrated History*, New England Library, London, 1979.

Hunt, J., and F. Hunt, *Peeps into Nisterland: A Guide to the Children's Books of Ernest Nister*, Casmelda, Chester, 2006.

Krahé, H.E., 'The Importance of Being Ernest Nister', trans. and ed. S. Fraser, *Phaedrus* XIII, 1988, pp. 73–90.

Lindberg, S.G., 'Mobiles in Books: Volvelles, Inserts, Pyramids, Divinations, and Children's Games', trans. W.G. Mitchell, *The Private Library*, 3rd ser., vol. II, no. 2, 1979, pp. 49–82.

Montanaro, A.R., *Pop-Up and Movable Books: A Bibliography*, Scarecrow Press, Metuchen NJ, 1993.

Speaight, G., 'Harlequinade Turn-ups', *Theatre Notebook*, vol. XLIV, no. 2, 1991, pp. 70–84.

About the contributors

Dr Anna Caughey is a Lecturer in Old and Middle English at Keble College, Oxford. Her primary research interests are in the representation of masculinity, knighthood and chivalry in both medieval and contemporary literature. She is currently completing a chapter on the quest-narrative in Tolkien's writing for the *Blackwell Companion to J.R.R. Tolkien*, forthcoming in 2014.

Dr David Clark is a Senior Lecturer at the University of Leicester. He teaches Old and Middle English literature and researches both medieval literature and its reception in contemporary children's fiction and film.

Hannah Field is a D.Phil. candidate in English at Somerville College, Oxford. Her doctoral research centres on nineteenth-century movable books for children.

Dr Carolyne Larrington is a Supernumerary Fellow and Tutor in Medieval English at St John's College, Oxford. Her main areas of research are Old Norse–Icelandic literature and Arthurian literature.

Dr Diane Purkiss is Fellow and Tutor in Early Modern English at Keble College, Oxford.

Index